THE
AMERICAN
AIRPORT

THE
AMERICAN
AIRPORT

Geza Szurvoy

MBI

First published in 2003 by MBI Publishing Company, Galtier Plaza, Suite 200, 380 Jackson Street, St. Paul, MN 55101-3885 USA

MBI Publishing Company titles are also available at discounts in bulk quantity for industrial or sales-promotional use. For details write to Special Sales Manager at Motorbooks International Wholesalers & Distributors, Galtier Plaza, Suite 200, 380 Jackson Street, St. Paul, MN 55101-3885 USA

ISBN 0-7603-1242-7

On the front cover: Los Angeles International Airport's most recognized image is the Theme Building, erected in 1963. It looks like a space ship that has just touched down from Hollywood or outer space. It houses a restaurant that has just been restored. It is flanked by the airport's new tower which has the letters LAX imaginatively included in its exterior design.

On the back cover: (*bottom left*) The terminal that most caught the popular imagination in the Jet Age was TWA's futuristic looking terminal at JFK, completed in 1963. In spite of its appearance, it was scaled for propliners and had an old-fashioned horizontal layout that was problematic throughout its active service. (*top right*) Washington National Airport got too crowded in the 1950s to keep its sweeping foyer free. Check-in counters took over the space, but passengers and visitors could still stroll out onto the balcony to watch the airplanes come and go. (*bottom right*) The International Arrivals Building became a symbol of JFK and was used in many ads, including this one for Convair's newest jet.

On the frontispiece: A restored Continental Airlines DC-3 recreates the past in front of Houston Hobby Airport Art Deco terminal. *Mike Fizer*

On the title page: This aerial survey shot of Chicago's Midway Airport shows that it was completely hemmed in by its neighborhood, making any runway expansion impossible. This situation required a second airport for Chicago, which it got with the development of O'Hare.

Photo sources: Atlanta Hartsfield International Airport: 144; Boston Public Library: 15, 16, 19, 31, 61, 63, 85, 147; Cheyenne Municipal Airport: 131; Chicago Airport Authority: 103; College Park Aviation Museum: 9, 23, 32; Cradle of Aviation Museum: 30, 44; Dallas/Fort Worth International Airport: 125; Denver International Airport: 140, 151, 154; Ezra Stoller, ESTO: 127 Houston Airport System: 111; JFK-IAT: 150; Kansas City, Missouri Aviation Department: 129; Los Angeles World Airports: cover, 37; Metropolitan Washington Airport Authority: 86, 87, 96, 121, 130; Museum of Flight, Seattle, Washington: 10, 12-18, 20, 21, 24, 26, 27, 29, 32, 34, 35, 36, 40, 41, 45, 47, 49, 50, 52, 53, 56-60, 62, 64, 67, 68, 70, 72, 73, 88, 93, 95, 98, 100, 104, 106, 108, 109, 113-115, 126-128, 133, 136, 137, 139, 150 (courtesy Addison Thompson), 152; Oakland International Airport: 122; San Francisco Airport Museum: 23, 69; San Francisco International Airport: 141, 143, 145; St. Louis International Airport: 25, 38, 118, 119; US Navy: 153; all other images from private collections

Edited by Steve Gansen
Designed by Chris Fayers

Printed in Hong Kong

CONTENTS

Introduction

Dick Merrill had plenty to be pleased about as he approached Byrd Field, the grass pasture at Richmond, Virginia, on a starry summer evening in 1928. He had been barnstorming for years in a beat-up Curtiss Jenny left over from World War I, but had recently been accepted to fly the U.S. Mail. He was in a big, brassy Pitcairn Mailwing, an open-cockpit biplane like his ancient Jenny, but an electrifying thoroughbred compared to it.

The lights identifying Byrd Field came into view and Merrill eased the Pitcairn onto final approach. But instead of throttling back he smoothly added full power and roared down the strip of grass with only feet to spare. He pulled up sharply into a wingover to make sure he had caught everyone's attention. Then came a dazzling series of loops and rolls and another low pass before the Pitcairn gently kissed the grass and the U.S. Mail from Atlanta arrived.

More than three decades later, on a balmy October afternoon, a sleek 118-passenger Douglas DC-8 jetliner approached Miami International Airport in Florida. It was Eastern Airlines Flight 601 four hours out of New York and was vectored onto final approach and cleared to land. The giant silver jet was perfectly stabilized and touched down light as a feather, effortlessly rolling to a stop with room to spare on the 8,000-foot concrete runway. The jet taxied in, the passengers disembarked, and then, reluctantly, its pilot, Captain Dick Merrill, walked off into retirement.

In one pilot's working life, aviation had gone from the stick and canvas Jennies to globe-spanning jetliners. The flying fields they needed for departure and to which they always had to return had undergone an equally remarkable transformation. They progressed from the farmer's pasture chosen from the air when the gas was getting low, to 10,000-acre, all-weather Washington Dulles International Airport with 12,000-foot concrete runways that could handle jetliners arriving nonstop from Europe and 25 million passengers a year.

This is the story of those flying fields. As aviation celebrates its first century of flight, this book traces the development of the American airport from the Wright Brothers' first field of flying to the $9 billion post-millenium refurbishment program of New York City's John F. Kennedy International Airport. It offers a multidisciplinary look at airports, focusing largely on the major trends and developments. It examines a blend of operational, financial, architectural, and social variables that create the airports of each era.

Airports don't stand alone. They are an integral part of our national aviation infrastructure and are best examined in that context. Airports rarely lead. They respond to, and at best they anticipate the needs of their users. To understand airports, we must look at the needs that created them and trace how these needs changed over the years.

The American Airport is chronological in organization. The first chapter examines the emergence of the first airports and looks at how and why they came to be as aviation passed through its first freewheeling few years, when it seemed to be a miracle and was largely a form of entertainment. It looks at the effects of World War I on the growth of airports and the results of the rapid technological advances in aviation that began to transform flying into a promising industry. It tells of the airmail's catalytic role in airport development, and it identifies a surprising number of pioneering pastures that live on as major airports today.

The second chapter covers the period when aviation and airports became sufficiently complex to warrant regulation. It follows the effect on airport development of Charles Lindbergh's transatlantic solo flight in 1927, which unleashed an aviation craze that expected an airplane in every garage and demanded an airport in every town. This period saw the responsibility for creating and financing public airports placed firmly in local, municipal hands and led to enthusiastic airport building as well as serious financial pressures.

The third chapter traces the history of airports through the Great Depression to the eve of World War II. Ironically, the need to put armies of the unemployed to work at simple, labor intensive projects led to a major expansion of airports through federally funded runway and terminal construction schemes. This precedent brought the federal government into partnership with local authorities and established joint responsibility for airport development, a structure that survives today.

This period saw the emergence of many of our best known airports and the creation of the revolutionary DC-3, the breakthrough which proved that air transportation could become a viable industry in its own right and survive without air-mail subsidies. This was the birth of modern air transportation, and it brought challenging new demands on airport development. The creation of Washington National Airport and LaGuardia Airport, the two airports that redefined airport standards at the end of the 1930s, is traced.

The fourth chapter addresses the cataclysmic effect of World War II on aviation and airport development and covers the golden years of the propliners. During this time aviation became a system of mass transportation with the attendant effect on airports. Idlewild, Chicago-Midway, St Louis Lambert Field, Los Angeles, Miami, San Francisco, and may other airports came into their own.

The last chapter opens with the arrival of the Jet Age and the jetports it brought. Washington Dulles, the first airport designed specifically to be a jetport, JFK, Dallas/Fort Worth, Los Angeles International Airport, Atlanta Hartsfield and others are examined in the context of the airline industry's wild roller-coaster transition to deregulation. The chapter ends with the present, when airports are undergoing a renaissance of sorts as our continuously increasing demand for air travel coexists with a newfound sense of aesthetics that expects nothing less than the signature air terminal, such as Denver International Airport and JFK's Terminal 4.

A century of history may seem little to look back on, especially for an industry forever looking to the future. But, as an old, bold flight instructor once told me, "It's not how many hours of flying you have in your logbook that matters. It's what you've done with them." The coming chapters will show that the American airport has used its first century well.

Acknowledgments

It would have been impossible to write *The American Airport* without assistance from many sources. Most important for telling the story in popular terms was the background provided by the excellent scholarly books and doctoral dissertations on various aspects of the topic.

I am chiefly indebted to the following works: *America's Airports: Airfield Development, 1918-1947,* by Janet R. Daly Bednarek (Texas A&M University Press, 2001); *Building for Air Travel: Architecture and Design for Commercial Aviation,* ed. John Zukowsky (The Art Institute of Chicago and Prestel-Verlag, 1996); *Airport Planning and Management,* 4th ed., by Alexander T. Wells, (McGraw Hill, 2000); "What Can't Go Up Can't Come Down: The History of American Airport Policy, Planning, and Design," by David Philip Brodherson, Ph.D. dissertation, Cornell University, 1993; "The Invention of Airports: A Political, Economic, and Technical History of Airports in the United States, 1919-1939," by Deborah G. Douglas, Ph.D. dissertation, University of Pennsylvania, 1996; "Leaving on a Jet Plane: Commercial Aviation, Airports, and Post-Industrial American Society, 1933-1970," by Douglas G. Karsner, Ph.D. dissertation, Temple University, 1993; and "Technology and the Terminal: St. Louis' Lambert Field, 1925-1974," by Charles Clifton Bonwell, Ph.D. dissertation, Kansas State University, 1975.

I also received invaluable assistance, photography, archival material, and advice from the dedicated staffs of many museums, airport authorities, libraries, and other organizations. I would particularly like to thank my good friends, Katherine Williams and Dennis Parks at the Museum of Flight, Seattle, Washington. The museum's excellent photo archives and collection once again came through to make a major contribution.

I am also greatly indebted to Catherine W. Allen, director, College Park Aviation Museum; Christine Harris, librarian, San Francisco Airport Museums; Chap Solomon, San Francisco International Airport; Jay Berkowitz, photographer, Los Angeles World Airports; Dan Curtin, Chicago Airport Authority; Charlene Whitney, Port Authority of New York and New Jersey; Barbara Margulis and Janice Holden, JFK International Air Terminal, LLC; Chris Carter, photographer, Denver International Airport; Tom Sullivan, Metropolitan Washington Airport Authority; Craig Clayton, Houston Airport System; Joshua Stoff, curator, and Glenn Appel, Cradle of Aviation Museum; the staff at the Boston Public Library Photo Archives; Star Ormand, Dallas–Fort Worth Airport; Barbara Platt, Massachusetts Port Authority; Marybeth Yarnell, Wichita, Kansas; and Marcia Hall, Atlanta Hartsfield International Airport.

I'd also like to thank Dick Gariepy of Barre, Massachusetts, for access to his father's American Airways memorabilia; my close friend and collaborator, Martin Berinstein, for his generous photo support for this book; and Steve Gansen and the folks at MBI Publishing for their patience, good humor, and assistance.

Chapter One
Pick a Pasture

On September 17, 1911, Calbraith Perry Rogers, a husky, broad faced young man fond of cigars, rose early and went to the racetrack at Sheepshead Bay on Long Island, New York. He hoped to win a large sum of money, but not by betting on the horses. With Orville Wright's signature barely dry on his pilot's license, he was after the $50,000 Hearst Prize for the first coast-to-coast

In this rare photograph, a Waco glides to a landing in a field in the Midwest in the early 1920s. Any dry, level patch of pasture land could serve as an airfield. The addition of a wooden hangar or two was the first step to turning an occasionally used plot into a permanent airfield.

Glenn Curtiss, the Wrights' chief competitor in America, wins the $10,000 Scientific American prize in his *June Bug* on July 4, 1908. Curtiss started to fly from his hometown of Hammondsport in upstate New York. Later, the organization he created constructed airports throughout the United States.

flight across the United States, to be completed in 30 days or less.

The racetrack at Sheepshead Bay was pressed into service in the manner of the day to serve as Rogers' airport of departure. His ultimate goal was another popular form of impromptu airfield, a sandy beach, in Long Beach, California, over 4,000 miles away along his intended route. As he clambered into the exposed pilot's perch astride the lower wing of his flimsy Wright Flyer, named the *Vin Fiz* after his sponsor's grape juice, Long Beach must have seemed further than the moon.

In between lay the airfields of his age: countless pastures, fairgrounds, racetracks, municipal parks, the lawns of private estates, parade grounds, sports fields, and, for the alarmingly frequent occasions when his engine would blow up in flight, the flattest piece of real estate under his wing. Rogers hopscotched across the continent following the railroad tracks for the lack of aeronautical charts. Sometimes he made it to the day's planned destination, but when he got lost or the cantankerous *Vin Fiz* suddenly decided to have a nervous breakdown, he had to find a suitable field along the way. Crashes en route held him up for days, but they never deterred him.

The big prize eluded Rogers, for his ordeal took 84 days instead of the prescribed 30. Seriously injured in the last crackup near his destination, he strapped his crutches to the wings as soon as he could get out of bed and continued on his way. When he alighted at last on the sands of Long Beach and dipped the *Vin Fiz*'s wheels in the Pacific's soothing surf, he was surely a winner

A rare photograph of Calbraith Perry Rogers touching down in the *Vin Fizz* at the Kellogg Ranch, in Pomona, California, on the next-to-last leg of the first coast-to-coast aerial crossing of America. It took Rogers 89 days and he survived numerous crashes en route.

despite missing out on the generosity of William Randolph Hearst. A year later, exhibiting the *Vin Fiz* over the water off Long Beach to commemorate his earlier triumph, he collided with a seagull and became one of aviation's first bird-strike fatalities.

Today, New York's John F. Kennedy International Airport stands near the onetime racetrack on Sheepshead Bay, and Long Beach's John Wayne Airport is but a stone's throw from the strip of sand where the *Vin Fiz* completed its transcontinental trek.

A widebody jet with over 400 passengers on board can make the trip between those two airports nonstop in four and a half hours. It would be rewarding, through some form of alchemy, to take Cal Rogers on that ride.

By 1911 the airplane hadn't progressed technologically to the point of being suitable or useful for regular cross-country flying, but was increasingly capable of sustained flight over a local area, staying within easy reach of its point of departure in case of

A poster issued by Cal Rogers' sponsor, the Vin Fizz grape juice company, traces his epic crossing of the United States. He wasn't deterred by the lack of airports along the way, making use of any suitable field.

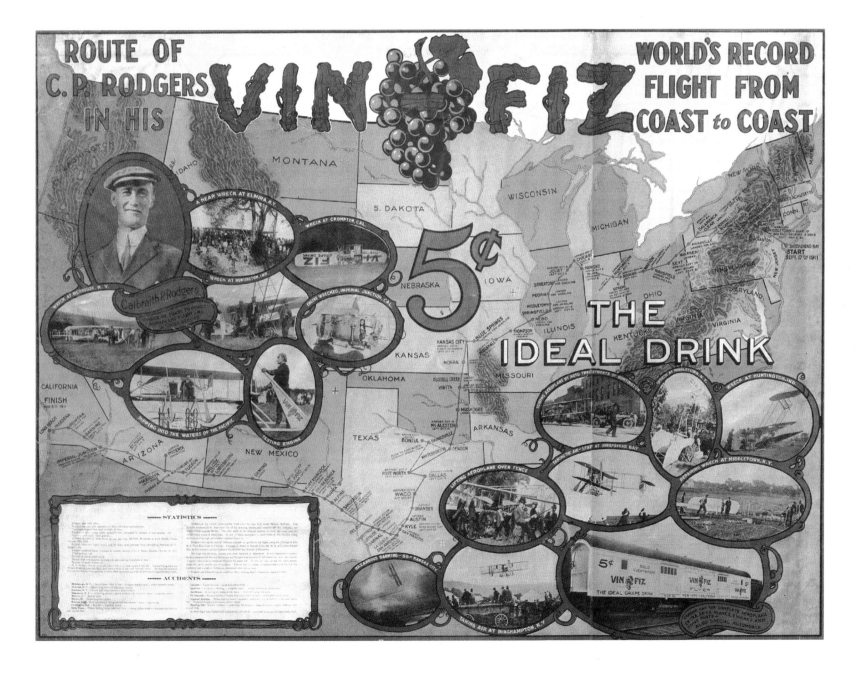

The Wright Flyer gets a workout above Huffman Prairie. During 1935, the Wrights remained airborne as long as 38 minutes and learned to fly "figure eights" with confidence.

trouble aloft. A growing number of aviation pioneers flocked to this preposterous, exhilarating, dangerous, yet increasingly plausible new frontier.

For a population barely out of the 19th century, the airplane was a more stunning and less comprehensible achievement than the landings on the moon would be to the technologically savvy society of the 1960s and 1970s. They had to see the miracle to believe it, and the aviation pioneers, chronically shorter on funds than enthusiasm, needed some way to commercialize their new cause to afford the costs of expanding its limits. And so it came to be that aviation's first commercially successful foray into mainstream society took the form of that quintessentially American economic activity: entertainment.

The airshow extravaganza took its rightful place alongside the traveling circus, the racetrack, the ball field, and the county fair, when every show was live and the only way to see it was to be there. The upstart aerial daredevils competed fiercely for the spectators' attention with bearded ladies, lion tamers, thoroughbreds, Ty Cobb, and prizewinning heifers. Some, like Lincoln Beachey, the first American to loop the loop, were content to be aerial circus performers. Others, like Beachey's employer and fellow display pilot, Glenn Curtiss, funded pioneering research and development with their airshow stunts. And as they spread their wings across the nation, more often than not sending their airplanes to the next gig dismantled and loaded on a freight train, they all needed fields of flying.

Most of the early airfields were merely fields of convenience, the most suitable areas of flat ground for the flying circus passing through town. But increasingly there was a need for permanent airfields, where systematic research and development could be conducted, aspiring aviators could be given flying instruction, and the barnstorming troupes could lick their wounds and concoct and polish the next season's thrills. And the Wright brothers' hard-earned success in convincing a skeptical U.S. Army to at least systematically examine the airplane's war-

waging potential soon led to the establishment of the nation's first military airfields.

Local pride, conflicting definitions, and hazy records often obscure rightful claims to first achievements. But if an airport is defined as "a place set aside primarily for the purpose of conducting regular, sustained flights," it can be safely said that America's first airport was Huffman Prairie Flying Field, established by the Wright brothers eight miles outside of Dayton, Ohio, in 1904.

Following their four epic hops under power across the sands of Kitty Hawk on December 17, 1903, the Wrights decided they needed a more permanent location closer to home to perfect their invention. Local banker Torrence Huffman generously allowed them to use a 100-acre dairy pasture he owned, known as

A Farman at Dominguez Airfield near Los Angeles in 1910 misses the spot landing target square. The balloon behind it represents 130 years of aviation history that had passed by then, including distance flights of hundreds of miles borne on the wind.

The Dominguez Aviation Meet was the first aviation meet in America. It gave over 250,000 residents of Los Angeles their first look at an airplane. Dominguez Field was the first airfield in the country built specifically to stage airshows.

Huffman Prairie, where they erected a permanent hangar and rolled out the new, improved version of their historic machine.

Immediately they encountered problems that would be familiar to future airport managers. They had to regularly chase off animals threatening to interfere with flying operations; in the Wrights' case, cows and horses competing for the pasture. More seriously, the field proved to be too small to comfortably meet their flying needs. They didn't always have enough room to face into the wind on takeoff, and inconveniently planted rows of trees at the edge of the field caused treacherous downdrafts under certain conditions.

But, like so many airport managers to come, the Wrights made do with the restrictions and achieved their goals. To overcome the lack of room to safely attain flying speed in the space available in calm conditions and light winds, they built an ingenious catapult powered by a 1,600-pound weight to accelerate them along the portable 60-foot track they used as a runway. In their first year of operations they made 105 takeoffs and landings, flew for as long as five minutes and eight seconds, covered distances as much as three miles, and learned to circle.

The following season the Wrights fully mastered the basics of fight. On the 46th flight of the year Wilbur Wright flew for over 38 minutes, circled the airfield about 30 times, and covered over 24 miles. The brothers could even fly at will the maneuver that best proves basic control, the figure eight. They were ready to commercialize the Flyer, and wouldn't fly for the next two years as they meticulously prepared their marketing campaign. Huffman Prairie had served its purpose. Though no longer an airfield today, it retains its links to aviation as a small, indistinct patch of Wright Patterson Air Force Base, and has been recently revived as an important national landmark.

Over the next decade developments in Europe and the United States gave aviation the critical mass that launched the air display movement and the first organized attempts to manufacture aircraft and teach people to fly. The Wright Flyer went into production in 1908 and was soon joined in the air by the Curtiss Pusher, an outstanding compact design by Glenn Curtiss, the wiry, business savvy, speed-obsessed motorcycle pioneer turned aviator.

Frenchman Louis Bleriot's famed *Bleriot* monoplane, first across the English Channel, also made its appearance in America, shamelessly built and sold in a knock-off version by the Queen Aeroplane Company of New York City and other U.S. entrepreneurs unimpressed by royalty demands from across the Atlantic. Unknown backyard tinkerers Bill Boeing, Glenn Martin, Clyde Cessna, and others were trying their luck with their own designs. And all this activity led to the establishment of the first permanent airports across the country.

In the Washington, D.C., area the Wrights' demonstration flights to sell their airplane to the army largely took place at Fort Myers, Virginia, but it was unsuitable for a permanent field. On a flight after the trials were complete, a fine square field was spotted at College Park, Maryland, and was pressed into service in 1909 as the army's first airport. College Park Airport is a national landmark today and the oldest continuously serving airport in the country. Within a few years Langley Field and Bolling Field also became important army airfields.

The aircraft types over Dominguez Field in 1910 represent every significant U.S. and European make of the time. The Wrights' secretive, time-consuming development of their airplane after their first flight left the field open to other pioneers. The Europeans, who received enthusiastic official support, made greater headway in the early years.

Boston's residents saw their first airplane in September 1910 when Englishman Claude Graham White took off in his Bleriot from nearby Squantum during the first Harvard Boston Aviation Meet and flew two round trips over Boston to claim the Boston Globe's $10,000 special prize. Squantum's open grounds were pressed into temporary service as an airfield for the Harvard Boston Aviation Meets.

Above: A candid shot of Wilbur Wright making an adjustment to the rigging of a Flyer at the 1910 Harvard Boston Aviation Meet. The field is little different from the grass fields serving thousands of sport flyers today.

Right: Glenn Martin taxies in a Martin TT on floats at North Island in San Diego, California, in 1914. The hangars are inspired by the classic boathouse of the time. Glenn Martin went on to build the flying boats for Pan American that played an important part in conquering the Pacific. North Island Naval Air Station is home to navy carriers today and an important land base for navy aircraft.

In the New York area the flat agricultural lands of Hempstead Plains on Long Island became a favorite haunt for flyers to stake out flying fields. Glenn Curtiss flew here in 1909 from Mineola and would return to establish a permanent field and airplane factory. The Moisants, famous for their touring air troupe, opened the Moisant Flying School in 1911 on Hempstead Plains.

Glenn Curtiss' home field was in his hometown of Hammondsport, in upstate New York, where he also used the local lake to experiment with aircraft on pontoons.

Cicero Field was Chicago's first field of flying, soon outgrown and superceded by nearby Ashburton Field, home of the Aeroclub of Illinois. In St. Louis, Missouri aviation pioneers Jannus and Benoist set up shop at Kinlock Field to produce their own designs. Among them was a tiny, two-seat flying boat which became America's first scheduled airliner when Benoist and Jannus went to Florida to launch the experimental St. Petersburg-Tampa Airboat Line in 1914. It was the first to offer scheduled service and used the commercial jetties at its two destinations for terminals.

In San Antonio, Texas, the army turned the parade ground at Fort Sam Houston into the Lone Star State's first airfield as an experiment and then leased it as winter quarters and a flying school to the Stinson family's flying circus, centered around teenager Katherine Stinson, the fourth licensed woman pilot in the United States.

When Pancho Villa, the Mexican freedom fighter or brigand (depending on the observer's point of view), started taunting his northern neighbors once again in 1916, the army wanted its field back. The First Aero Squadron under Captain Benjamin Foulois, who learned to fly at College Park, was soon hot on Villa's trail, but the Stinsons had to find a new airfield. Katherine Stinson's brother, Eddie, hopped onto one of the school's Wright Flyers and scouted out a new 750 acre location nearby which the Stinson's leased and which lives on today as Stinson Field.

California's first airfield was opened in 1910 atop Dominguez Hill, halfway between San Pedro Harbor and Los Angeles, where Compton stands today.

Known alternately as Dominguez Field and Aviation Park, it was America's first airfield established specifically from which to stage airshows. It was inspired by the highly successful 1909 air meet at Rheims, France, where Glenn Curtiss narrowly won the Gordon Bennett Cup for the fastest speed around a prescribed course. Curtiss' victory had gained high visibility throughout the United States and played an important role in stirring up popular enthusiasm for the miracle of human flight.

Dominguez Field was chosen by Charles Willard, a Glenn Curtiss protégé, who selected it, among other reasons, because it was atop a hill which prevented freeloaders, who didn't pay the admission fee, from seeing much of the flying which mostly

A view of San Diego Airport in 1913. Located across from North Island, it was one of the first airports in the country. Later the airfield was home to the Ryan Aircraft Corporation, builders of Charles Lindbergh's *Spirit of St. Louis*, and today it lives on as Lindbergh Field serving San Diego.

The Michigan State Fairgrounds are pressed into service to host the 1911 Detroit Aviation Meet. This was a common arrangement before towns and cities began to establish permanent airports.

Below: A long line of hangars at Dominguez Field housed the many participants of the 1912 Aviation Meet. Mechanics were becoming as important as pilots to the success of aviation. The maze of structural wires reveals why mechanics were also called "riggers" in the early days.

took place a few dozen feet above the ground. Dominguez Field was laid out as a hexagonal track with straightaways suitable for closed-circuit air racing. It was overlooked by a grandstand capable of accommodating 26,000 spectators. A row of wooden hangars was erected in the middle of the field, and during an airshow it even boasted a field first-aid station grandly dubbed a hospital. The 1910 air meet was a spectacular success, attracting over 270,000 spectators during eleven days, most of whom saw flight for the first time in their lives.

Nine months later, on a blustery afternoon in September 1910 it was the turn of the residents of Boston, Massachusetts to have their first brush with flight. The crowds who gathered around Boston Light heard a faint, strange buzz coming from above. The tiny, kite-like apparition they found crawling toward them when they looked up was the first airplane any of them had ever seen—a miraculous vision at a time when the motor car was a rarity among the thousands of horse-drawn carriages on Boston's streets.

The airplane was a Bleriot monoplane, flown by the young Englishman Claude Graham White taking part in the Harvard Boston Aviation Meet at nearby Squantum, his point of departure. The first such meet of its kind on America's east coast, it brought together a Who's Who of the first aviators and flying machines: the Wright brothers, Glenn Curtiss, Graham White with the Bleriot and a Farman two seater in which he gave scores of rides, and White's pioneering compatriot, A. V. Roe, with two of his intriguing triplanes, both of which he wrecked.

The crowds flocked to see them. Over 250,000 turned up for the 13-day event, and a million more saw Graham White's flight over Boston. Mayor John "Honey Fitz" Fitzgerald and Massachusetts Lieutenant Governor Frothingham took their first airplane rides, flying with Graham White. President Taft demurred only because his great bulk exceeded the weight of Graham White's Farman. Also present were Franklin Delano Roosevelt and several young spectators who went on to open Boston's first airport in 1923.

While entertaining the crowds was glamorous, the most perceptive aviation pioneers also focused on attempting to commercialize the flying machine.

The Wrights had the edge on selling airplanes to the army, so Glenn Curtiss decided to try his luck with the navy and went to San Diego to make his pitch. He established a flying school on North Island. Today North Island Naval Air Station is one of the navy's most prestigious air bases and home ports for its aircraft carriers. Another airfield that soon started up across from North Island is now known as San Diego's Lindbergh Field.

In 1911 in a marshy pasture outside of Salt Lake City called Basque Flats, a cinder-covered landing strip was established for airshow performances long before the town became an important transcontinental airmail stop. The strip eventually became Woodward Field, and today it is Salt Lake City International Airport.

By 1914 there were about 20 civilian flying fields in America that were more or less permanent. They were privately owned, minimally improved flat patches of real estate, blissfully free of any government interference. Most sprouted a ramshackle hangar or two to shelter the delicate kite-like flying machines so easily damaged by the elements. They featured little else beyond some rudimentary fuel storage and maintenance arrangements.

Curiously, but understandably for those days preceding the widespread ownership of personal automobiles, most flying fields were easily accessible by some form of public transportation, usually a train or tramline. The Wrights commuted by tram every day to Huffman Prairie Flying Field from their home and workshops in downtown Dayton. College Park, Maryland, was close to a railroad to Washington, D.C., and airshow attendees at Dominguez Field could ride a train from Los Angeles to within a half mile of their destination.

The Benoist flying boat was a successful early commercial airplane. All it needed for an airfield was a dock and a stretch of calm water. In 1914 a small fleet of Benoist flying boats established the world's first scheduled airline service between Tampa and St. Petersburg, Florida. This Benoist is giving joy rides over Nantucket, Massachusetts.

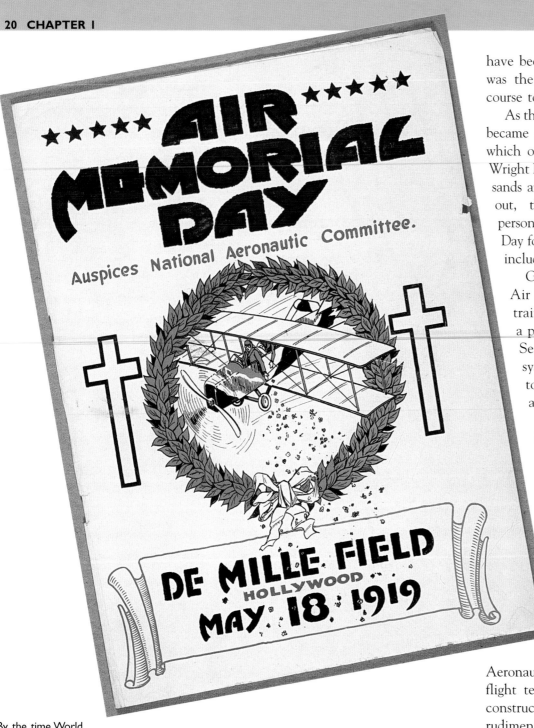

By the time World War I was over, America had its first fighter aces and the airplane was transformed from a form of entertainment into an effective war machine, with promise for a civilian future and a need for airports.

have been achieved as fast in a world at peace. It was the catalyst that firmly set the airplane on course to realize its vast potential.

As the war progressed and America's involvement became increasingly likely, the U.S. armed forces, which only recently were so reluctant to take the Wright Flyer seriously, needed airplanes by the thousands and pilots to fly them. When the war broke out, the military had about 1,300 aviation personnel, of whom 33 were pilots. By Armistice Day four years later, it would have about 160,000, including over 12,000 pilots.

Glenn Curtiss obliged the army's fledgling Air Service with the Curtiss Jenny, a two-seat training biplane that would go on to become a postwar barnstorming legend. And the Air Service set out to create the country's first systematically organized airports, primarily to provide facilities at which to train its aspiring airmen.

In 1916 the Air Service established Langley Field in Hampton, Virginia, its first purpose-designed permanent air base. For the first time an architect was hired to design a U.S. airfield. He was Albert Kahn, a highly regarded industrial architect who, for the first time, professionally addressed issues of airfield grading, drainage, hangar structure and location, and maintenance and supply support requirements.

Langley was also designated to be a research base, to be operated together with the recently formed National Advisory Committee for Aeronautics (NACA) for aeronautical research and flight testing. Concurrently with the decision to construct Langley, the Air Service also established rudimentary airfields in New York, Texas, Hawaii, and the Philippines.

As the need for additional training fields became acute, the Air Service turned once again to Albert Kahn, who created a generic airfield design capable of supporting up to 200 aircraft, sufficient to equip four air squadrons. In the interest of time and cost savings, Kahn's design was minimalist, largely borrowed from the airfield standards of the Royal Canadian Air Force,

The first generation of aviators' exuberant antics increasingly fired the popular imagination, but across the Atlantic the flying circus was about to turn deadly serious. Europe was on the brink of World War I, and the airplane was about to become its star weapon. The war unlocked massive government resources on all sides to give aviation a concentrated technological boost that could not

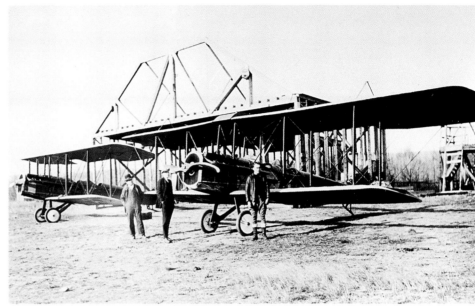

which was by then heavily involved in training Allied pilots for deployment primarily to France.

Kahn's design was centered around a square field measuring one mile on each side. A field of this size provided an ample ground run and sufficient obstacle clearance for takeoffs and landings in any direction the compass rose. It allowed aircraft to always take off and land straight into the wind regardless of the direction from which it happened to be blowing. This was an important consideration, since aircraft with tail skids and tail wheels are unstable on the ground because of their tendency to weathervane. They are much more sensitive to crosswinds than aircraft with nose wheels, a configuration that didn't become standard until World War II. The windsock came into use to indicate wind direction for pilots both preparing to take off and land.

Kahn specified rudimentary drainage standards, a requirement well understood from road and park construction. Experiments commenced with airfield markers, mostly using whitewash. Marking was critically important to help overcome one of the most difficult challenges novice pilots face to this day, the task of finding an unpaved airfield from the air, nestled among all the other, similar fields surrounding it. The surest way to differentiate was by painting an enormous white circle in the middle of the field, a marker that became standard for decades.

The generic army airfield design specified 15 hangars along one edge, giving the airplanes instant access to the field. The hangars were of a size and construction that allowed unskilled builders to rapidly assemble them and take them apart without the need for special tools or heavy equipment. A special roof truss designed by Kahn allowed the hangars to be wide enough to store several aircraft in a space unhindered by internal columns. Living quarters and support facilities of similarly easy construction were erected in neat military lines behind the hangars.

The selection of the site for an airfield had to meet certain important considerations. The chosen site had to be near a suitable railhead and a good road network to meet the need for ground access for relatively high volumes of material, supplies, and personnel. On a higher level, if a proposed airfield's training function was a greater priority than its geographic location, sites with the best year-round weather were to receive the highest priority.

The typical training field had several auxiliary landing fields around it where students could practice takeoffs and landings without interfering with the main field's busy traffic, which at times could border on the chaotic. Normally there were also several emergency fields scattered throughout the flying area of a particular training field to accommodate the unreliable training machines prone to engine failure.

Above left: The Army Air Service sought to maintain its skills through reserve programs during the 1920s. Here tent hangars are used to assemble the Curtiss Jennies prior to maneuvers at Ashburn Field in Illinois.

Above: These hangars under construction were typical of the inexpensive wooden structures that were beginning to appear at permanent airfields throughout the country.

America's Oldest Active Airport

Following their first historic hops at Kitty Hawk, North Carolina, in 1903, the Wright Brothers quietly disappeared from public view. For years much of the world doubted if they had flown at all. They certainly had, but they retreated to secretively improve their invention until they felt it was perfected enough to be offered to the U.S. Government.

In 1908 the Wrights gave a series of demonstration flights, followed in 1909 by official tests in the Washington, D.C. area, mostly at Fort Myers, Virginia. Suitably impressed, the U.S. Army finally bought the Wright Flyer with the condition that the Wrights teach two army officers to fly it. The Wrights chose a field in College Park, Maryland, for the flying lessons.

Lieutenants Frederick Humphreys and Frank Lahm were the first student pilots to lift off from the newly established College Park Airfield in 1909. The field has been operating ever since, earning the honor of being America's oldest continuously operating airport.

Wilbur Wright declared Humphreys and Lahm full-fledged pilots after only three hours of flight training each. Wright also taught Lt. Benjamin Foulois to fly, who was soon off to chase Pancho Villa from the air on the Texas-Mexico border.

In 1911 the Signal Corps formally opened the U.S. Army's first Aviation School at College Park with two Wright Flyers and two Curtiss Pushers. Lieutenant Henry H. "Hap" Arnold, future commander of the U.S. Army Air Forces through World War II, was among the first instructors.

The army achieved several firsts, including the first release of a bomb from an airplane and the first firing of a machine gun from an airplane. Flight training proceeded successfully, but within two years the army concluded that it would be better served with training fields with weather that allowed year-round training, and closed its operation at College Park.

The airfield continued to thrive following the army's departure, providing a home for civilian operators. They included the Rex Smith Aeroplane Company, the National Aviation Company, and the Washington Aeroplane Companies who flew a mix of Wright, Curtiss, and Bleriot airplanes as well as some homegrown types. The airport was popular with the Washington elite for sport as well as the occasional practical trip. One of the pilots flying from the airport was Tony Jannus, who in 1914 launched the world's first airline, the St. Petersburg-Tampa Airboat Line.

In 1918 the government was back, designating College Park as Washington's airmail terminus for the mail runs initially to Philadelphia and New York. The operation lasted until 1921.

By then a weird, stubby-winged craft was seen at College Park huffing and puffing to spin a set of oversized propellers mounted above it. It was the Berliner brothers' first experimental helicopter. For several years it managed only minor, semi-controlled hops, but eventually it achieved the first successful controlled helicopter flight in the world. The flight was modest, attaining 15 feet in altitude and maneuvering within a 150-foot radius at up to 40 miles per hour, but it validated the theory of helicopter flight.

The government returned once again in 1927 when the Bureau of Standards selected College Park as its base for developing and testing radio navigation

Kahn's generic army airfield could be built in 60 days, and many were. By Armistice Day on November 11, 1918, the Air Service had over 20 training fields where most of America's first crop of combat-hardened flying aces had earned their wings.

Assumed to be temporary when they were built, several of these fields acquired permanent status as it became evident that the Air Service had become a force in its own right. Among them was Kelly Field, which would grow to serve the U.S. armed forces until the end of the 20th century and lives on in spirit at nearby Randolph and Lackland Air Force Bases. Others, such as Love Field in Dallas, Texas, would at various points pass into civilian hands and become important national airports.

By 1919 the Air Service had accumulated enough experience constructing and operating airfields to publish *Municipal Landing Fields for Air Service*, the first set of airport specification guidelines for cities and towns contemplating the construction of their own airports. In 1923 it was expanded into a circular titled *Airways and Landing Fields*, one of the first how-to guides for establishing an aviation infrastructure, including a detailed chapter on constructing airfields.

aids and avionics to achieve safe, reliable flight in instrument conditions. The first blind landing took place here in 1931, and the experiments culminated in 1934 in the first totally blind flight using radio nav aids to navigate and land, from College Park to Newark Airport in New Jersey. The landing system onboard, with its vibrating reed indicator, was the forerunner of the modern instrument landing system still in use today.

From then on, College Park became one of thousands of small general aviation fields. It lacked the room to expand to attract the large-scale commercial aviation businesses that were migrating to the larger and ever-growing airports that were beginning to sprout nationwide.

College Park Airport was managed from 1927 to 1959 by George Brickenhoff, whose Flying Service taught hundreds of student pilots to fly. It has since been run by a succession of Fixed Base Operators, including Brickenhoff's sons, and defended over the years by fiercely loyal weekend and general aviation pilots from the encroachment of developers.

In 1973, College Park Airport was bought by the Maryland-National Capital Park and Planning Commission, and in 1977 the airport was added to the National Register of Historic Places. Today it is both a historic site and operating airport. Its achievements are recognized in the 27,000-square-foot College Park

Aviation Museum on site, designed by the same firm that designed the National Air and Space Museum and several major airport projects. Its past is also evoked by the roll call of pilots who flew from here, including Orville and Wilbur Wright, Glenn Curtiss, Lincoln Beachey, Hap Arnold, Benjamin Foulois, Tony Jannus, and others.

A Wright Flyer lifts off from America's oldest continuously operating airport as the nation's first army fliers train for their pilot's wings.

In addition to these comprehensive technical guidelines *Airways and Landing Fields* stressed the need to place an airport where it was unlikely to be hemmed in by future development, and plan it with plenty of room for expansion. Aviation's dizzying pace of development in the coming years made such advice difficult to live up to at times, even with the most visionary attitude.

The Air Service recognized from its wartime experience that aviation's future lay in the ability to fly far beyond the scope of local hops, in order to peek across enemy lines. Its publications were

The hangars at Chanute Field in Rantoul, Illinois, are indistinguishable from the ones at Kelly Field in Texas. Designed by industrial architect Albert Kahn, they were one of the first purpose-designed airport structures.

By 1923 the Army Air Service had established a network of airways to guide the fledgling Airmail service. The system included lighting, which was first tried between Cheyenne, Wyoming, and Chicago. The stars on the map represent individual lights along a lighted airway. Each dotted circle represents an airport.

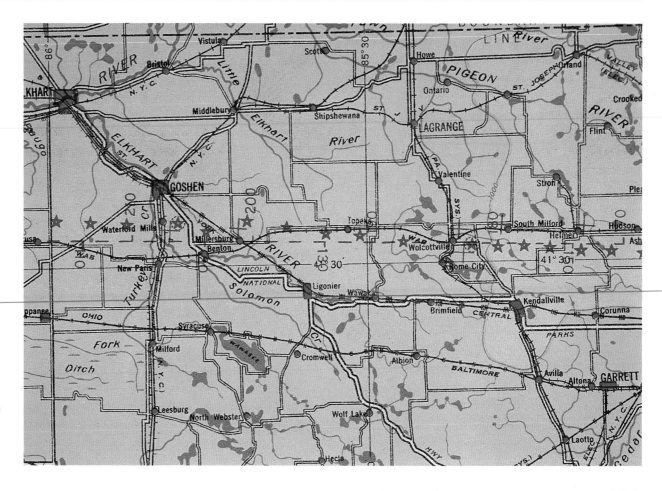

Below: This survey photograph shows the beginning of an airport at Paoli, Pennsylvania. The selected site is marked off in white ink from the adjoining farmland. Grading, surfacing with a suitable grass mix, and, if the job is done with attention to detail, drainage work will follow.

part of an ambitious postwar mission to establish a network of airports and airways across the country that would enable safe and seamless operation nationwide.

Concurrently with the Air Service's enthusiastic beginnings, another arm of the government developed a keen early interest in the airplane's possibilities. The United States Post Office Department was the first entity to see the airplane as a practical mode of point-to-point transportation, one that could potentially shave days off sending the mail coast to coast by train.

The idea of carrying mail by air had captivated some of the more forward-looking U.S. postal officials obsessed with the speed of mail delivery as early as 1912. Wider support was slow to come, given the early airplanes' severe limitations, but that attitude began to change when aircraft began to prove their worth in World War I. Impressed by the performance of aircraft in the war, Congress authorized

The first hangar erected at Lambert Field in St. Louis, Missouri, in 1920, was little more than a simple shed, but it gave enough protection from the elements to transient airmail pilots. Lambert Field later became a main TWA base and is still St. Louis' main airport.

modest funding for an experimental airmail service early in the war, prior to America's formal entry into the conflict. The Post Office was delighted, but now it found it impossible to get airplanes because the War Department had monopolized production.

To get around the problem, the Post Office boldly suggested that military pilots and aircraft carry the mail in exchange for the benefit of the cross-country flying experience they would gain by doing so. The War Department finally gave in, and it was agreed to set up the experiment between Washington, D.C., and New York City, with an interim stop in Philadelphia.

College Park, Maryland, lost out to the Washington Polo Grounds as the airmail experiment's terminus in the nation's capital because College Park was deemed too far from the central post office, but within a few months it would get another chance. In New York the landing strip at the Belmont Park race course was chosen, and

Bustleton Field in North Philadelphia served as the interim stop.

To great fanfare, personally watched by President Wilson, the experiment was launched on May 15, 1918. Army Curtiss Jennies departed both Washington and New York bearing sacks of commemorative mail. Apart from a navigational mishap by the pilot of the Washington-Philadelphia inaugural leg, which forced him down south of the capital on, of all places, a farm owned by the Postmaster General, the day went well.

The project was continued over the next three months with unexpected reliability, at which point the decision was made to make the airmail service permanent. The Post Office Department acquired its own aircraft, six Standard biplanes, and hired its own civilian pilots to take over from the Air Service pilots.

College Park, being a larger and more suitable airfield than the Polo Grounds, was selected as the Air Mail Service's Washington base. The newly

Another favorite airport layout in the early days was circular. It permitted takeoffs and landings in any direction, straight into the wind.

hired mail pilots were adventurers to a man, drawn from the ranks of the most flamboyant former army flyers and barnstormers. They set out with a missionary zeal that bordered on the insane to blaze the transcontinental airmail trail. The Post Office ruthlessly encouraged their brazen determination to let neither rain, nor sleet, nor snow stop them from getting through with the mail.

But the Post Office had a problem. It needed airports along the way—and had little funding to build and maintain any of them. The Air Service faced a similar predicament. In addition to wishing

to expand its reach nationwide following World War I, it wanted to maintain the proficiency of its reserve officers scattered throughout the country. It, too, needed airports to meet these missions, but severe postwar funding cutbacks forced it to retrench and put any thought of even the most modest base expansion program out of the question. Government funding for airport construction was not an option in this era of frugal federal rule, when most financing of public projects was still up to the states.

The Post Office and the Air Service followed similar tactics to get the airports they needed, and

The pilots were heroes to the kids of the day, attracting big crowds of them. A group of kids are thrilled to feel they are part of the scene as they are buffeted by a departing plane's propwash.

in doing so they set the pattern for U.S. airport development as civil aviation blossomed in the coming years. Their solution was to convince the local municipal authorities to build and pay for airports in their communities.

Their logic was sound. Popular infatuation with technology was becoming increasingly widespread. The rapid pace of scientific and industrial innovation cast a general mood of optimism across the country, and such progress was seen to offer great promise for solving society's ills. Many civic leaders were among the strongest advocates of technological progress. In their view, to ignore the opportunities it offered was to be left behind.

Many communities were particularly eager to be chosen as way stations on the evolving transcontinental airmail network. The speed of business mail was widely seen as a key competitive advantage. In the view of the strongest advo-

cates for aviation, to pass up the opportunity to be a direct stop on the airmail network would have been like choosing to forego high-speed internet capability today.

There was opposition, too, most often coming

As the airways fanned out across the nation and the airmail flights attempted to maintain tight schedules coast-to-coast to beat the surface mail, it became imperative to effectively and quickly exchange information between airports about weather conditions and the status of flights. Airport-to-airport radio communication in Morse code was quickly developed in the early 1920s. The Morse code sender became a cherished personal tool of virtuoso radio operators at airports everywhere.

Left: Henry Ford Airport was first to have paved runways, thus it became referred to as the Model Airport.

Engineering Laboratory and Airport
Ford Motor Company

Right: Henry Ford made the first effective American airliner, the Ford Trimotor, at Henry Ford Airport in Dearborn, Michigan. It was considered an advanced airport and had the first modern airline terminal, a simple, functional building with a modest second floor that could serve as a tower.

from those members of the community who wouldn't personally have a need to send their private correspondence by expensive airmail. So, when the question of funding a municipal airport advocated by civic leaders came to a community vote, projects were at times turned down. But on the balance, approvals outpaced rejections, even if some airport proposals took a year or two of lobbying by postal officials and civic leaders.

When a municipality encountered opposition, lacked the funds, or lacked a clear legal right to establish an airfield, it was common for local businessmen supportive of aviation to take the initiative. They joined forces, usually through the local chamber of commerce, to establish an airfield privately for their community, providing financing, land, and construction assistance on concessionary

terms. This was how what is now Gerald R. Ford Airport in Grand Rapids, Michigan, came into being. Many such airports were officially acquired by the municipality at a later date.

As early as 1920 the U.S. Post Office had put in place a skeleton network that reached from New York to San Francisco and enabled it to formally announce the opening of a transcontinental airmail system. Airfields along the route were spaced at approximately every 200 miles, the effective range of the mail planes. Among the major cities chosen to be the prime beneficiaries of airmail were Cleveland, Chicago, Des Moines, and Salt Lake City. Other stops were chosen mostly because of their convenience as refueling stops, such as Bellefonte, Pennsylvania; North Platte, South Dakota; Cheyenne, Wyoming; and Elko, Nevada.

Above: By the mid 1920s operators were experimenting with local air services and needed to establish the first rudimentary passenger service facilities. This simple airline office, photographed at a later date, was representative of most passengers' first experience with checking in for a flight. *Right:* As passenger services began to take hold, Dutchman Anthony Fokker's wood-winged trimotors, license-built in the United States, became the standard large airliner of the era. A highly publicized failure of the wooden wing and the appearance of the all-metal Ford Trimotor led to the end of the Fokkers.

Cheyenne, also an important transcontinental railway junction, was a vital technical stop for the airmail because of its location. It was the gateway to the low, wide passes through the Rocky Mountains that could provide the most direct safe passage between the peaks for the era's low-performance airplanes.

The transcontinental airmail's choice of route was largely dictated by the shortest practical path across the country, connecting those major cities that would provide the benefit of airmail to the greatest number of customers, most of whom were businesses. The idea was to establish spur lines to connect with the transcontinental route, and they weren't long in coming, prompting more communities to build airports for fear of being left out of the airmail loop. Detroit, Denver, and Los Angeles were particularly keen to be connected.

Opening day at Roosevelt field on Long Island, New York, in the 1920s, such occasions were major social events, drawing most of the local community.

By the mid-1920s the Post Office also had established a main north-south airmail route along the East Coast from the Northeast into Florida, which drew its own spur lines from the surrounding cities and towns.

The airmail service made two other important contributions at this early stage to the development of the nation's aviation infrastructure that had an effect on airport operations. In its race with the train, it realized that it had to fly day and night to significantly outpace the delivery of express surface mail. Thus, the airmail service pioneered cross-country night flying.

Navigation was the big challenge at night, and to overcome it, the airmail service developed the lighted airway. The first experimental segment was established along the Chicago-Cheyenne route, which had to be flown at night for mail that had left either New York or San Francisco in the morning to make it across the country nonstop.

Powerful electric beacons placed at frequent intervals along the route did the job in all but the worst conditions, and lighted emergency landing fields were established every 25 miles. The experiment forcefully made its point. The first nonstop transcontinental airmail made it across in 36 hours less than the fastest train-borne mail. Airway lighting was gradually expanded throughout the network and remained in use for many years until navigation by radio beam made it obsolete.

Chronically underfunded, the airmail service also had a need for a less expensive alternative to the teletype landline to communicate between airports to keep track of its mail planes and provide its pilots with crucial weather information for their next flight segments. It solved its problem by developing the first reliable radio communications network that linked its chain of airports.

The solution was somewhat accidental, because initially the airmail service set out to explore air-to-ground communications. When the bulk and unreliability of the airborne equipment became apparent, the service settled on perfecting the less ambitious option of airport-to-airport radio communication. The figure of the lonely airport manager-radio oper-

ator on the job seven days a week, twenty-four hours a day at some high desert refueling strip in the middle of nowhere became a national symbol of dedication to the march of progress.

The Army Air Service also pursued its mission to expand its reach and maintain flying proficiency in the face of severe peacetime budget and personnel cuts. It created the Air Service Reserve Flying Field program, aggressively pitching local officials of the larger population centers to fund airfields which could be used for civilian flying, but where reserve officers could also keep their skills sharp and provide reserve training for new pilots.

This is how Boston's first airport, Commonwealth Airport in east Boston was built in 1923. It was laid out on the tidal flats extending into Boston Harbor and required cinder-surfaced runways to enable airplanes to use the soggy ground. Its "T" layout was the first modern runway configuration, and it is also sometimes referred to as being the first hard-surfaced runway in the country. Today it has grown into Boston Logan International Airport.

While an appeal to patriotic duty held less sway over local communities in peacetime than the risk of being left behind by the airmail, several other cities built Air Service Reserve Flying Fields. Among them was Tuscon, Arizona, which, in 1919 became the first community in the country to establish an airfield approved by municipal legislation and funded by the municipality. This approach would soon become the standard for establishing public airfields. Reserve fields were also built in Pittsburgh, Pennsylvania; Seattle, Washington; Santa Monica, California; and Cincinnati, Ohio.

The Air Service also created the Model Airway program, assuming the responsibility in 1920 for developing a national infrastructure of airways for both military and civilian use. The Model Airway featured strategically placed emergency fields, airway ground markings, and lighting for night operations.

The first model airway linked Bolling Field in Washington, D.C., with McCook Field in Dayton, Ohio. As the Post Office embarked on its ambitious

Boston's airport, built on the tidal flats of east Boston in 1923, was one of the first airports with a modern runway layout. The surface was made of hard-packed cinders, necessitated by the soggy ground that required hardening to safely handle aircraft. Some consider these to be the first hard-surface runways in the nation.

San Francisco's first airfield was the army's Crissy Field at the Presidio, established in 1921. The famous San Francisco fog can be seen hovering in the background. Note the absence of the Golden Gate Bridge, which was not built until the following decade. The dotted line marks the boundaries of the airport.

(O-156-32-I-15)(7-12-27-12.00A)(12-3000) (Crissy Field, S.F. California.

Projected boundary of Flying Field.

Below: The hangars of College Park, Maryland, outside Washington, D.C., are seen through the feet of the pilot flying a Wright Flyer in 1912.

airmail program, it worked closely with the Air Service in laying the foundations of the country's airway system until the military relinquished this role in 1926.

The Post Office and the Air Service were not the only organizations to prompt the establishment of airfields in the first half of the 1920s. In fact, privately owned airfields continued to outnumber municipal fields during this period. Many were negligible, rough strips marked out by local enthusiasts and dreamers, but many were the private airports of a small but increasing number of emerging aviation businesses, including flying schools and clubs, aircraft manufacturers, the occasional air charter service, and even a budding airline or two.

To some extent the privately owned fields were another catalyst for the establishment of municipal airports. Local authorities could be wary of a private airfield, fearing that it could monopolize aviation to the detriment of the local community. Many municipalities responded to this perceived

An early navigation technique before the days of avionics was reading the signs painted on strategic structures along the popular airways. Here a pilot passes over a water tank that tells him the direction and distance to Chicago Municipal Airport. This pilot went on to fly DC-6s for National Airlines and perished in an accident due to mechanical failure over the Gulf of Mexico.

Below: A Wright Flyer over College Park, America's oldest continuously operating airfield, races a train passing along the rail line bordering the airfield. College Park was selected by the U.S. Army Air Service in 1909 as the location for training its first pilots.

threat by building a municipal field to serve the public interest.

By the mid 1920s over 80 of America's largest cities had airports, and about 50 of them were municipally owned. The airmail was a national success; over a dozen companies were engaged in building airplanes, scores of flying schools were training pilots, and the first airlines were beginning to offer their services to the public. Aviation had become newsworthy enough for most major city newspapers to employ full-time aviation correspondents.

Yet there was a complete absence of national rules, regulations, and standards governing the operation and construction of aircraft and the underlying infrastructure. Any ignorant, optimistic nut could concoct a flying machine in his back yard and kill himself in it. The barnstormers' crazy antics

Buffalo, New York, was the site of an important regional airport and another Curtiss Aerodrome. The Curtiss Company sought to provide a complete range of services in order to capture the largest share possible of the aviation market. It built airplanes, owned airports and service providers, performed air taxi operations, and offered flight instruction.

were also beginning to get tiresome and were giving aviation safety a bad name.

All that was about to change. Aviation had become too big and complex an industry to continue functioning at acceptable levels of public safety without any government oversight, and Congress decided to act. Its Air Commerce Act of 1926 would establish America's first sweeping set of regulatory standards for the coming air age.

Meanwhile, a lanky young Minnesotan was quietly preparing for an epic flight that would turn America's blossoming infatuation with aviation into a national hysteria and set off a boom in airport development.

Spectators lend a hand to prop a reluctant engine. By the mid 1920s over 80 of America's largest cities had airports, and hundreds of airplanes were flying thousands of hours performing a variety of tasks from flying the mail to carrying passengers.

Chapter Two
An Airport for Every Town

A Transamerican Airlines Fokker Trimotor prepares to leave Detroit Airport for Cleveland and on to Chicago. Passengers had been transferred from downtown Detroit in a company limousine. The terminal building is attached to the end of a large hangar. Note the tower.

Eddie Stinson was flying home to the family field in San Antonio, Texas, when his Wright Flyer suddenly began to vibrate alarmingly. Unnerved and on the verge of losing control, Stinson hastily plunked down the airplane on the first available patch of ground. When the dust settled and he looked around, he found himself in a graveyard.

A careful examination of the Flyer revealed that a bolt had failed in the elevator assembly. A few more minutes in the air, and the airplane would have disintegrated, most likely killing Stinson. But having calmed down after his escape, Eddie was not interested in what might have been. He just wanted to get home and was wondering where on earth he

OFFICIAL PROGRAM 25¢

1928 NATIONAL AIR RACES & AERONAUTICAL EXPOSITION LOS ANGELES SEPT. 8-16

could get a replacement part without a tedious land expedition, when a bolt holding down a coffin lid caught his attention. It was a perfect match, and Eddie happily winged his way home before anyone had time to notice he was overdue.

Eddie Stinson's experience was typical of the free-wheeling attitude to airplane design and maintenance in the early days, but by the mid 1920s, as aircraft were getting bigger and more powerful, many observers in and out of government were becoming concerned about the often reckless nature of this new world of aviation.

Flyers less lucky than Stinson were dying in droves. Two out of three barnstormers were perishing in crashes caused not only by their daredevil antics, but by poor aircraft design and even poorer maintenance that caused airframe and engine failures. Others were killed when they tried to teach themselves to fly in the absence of any requirements for instruction and pilot certification. Yet others bought the farm, as their contemporaries liked to put it, in bad weather, or trying to land at inferior, inadequately maintained airfields or on a poorly selected pasture of their choice.

Aviation's successes were also suggesting the need for some form of control over the industry. The airmail was demonstrating the feasibility of spanning the continent by air, reliably and on a schedule. Airplanes seating as many as a dozen passengers were beginning to make an appearance. Aviation was increasingly offering commercial services to the public, and Europe's more advanced, nationally supported airlines suggested a bright future. Borrowing bolts from coffins to keep an airplane flying would no longer do. Sad as it seemed to the most free spirited aviators, it was time for the government to weigh in with standards, regulations, and even a little financial support.

But big federal government was still in the future, and the Coolidge Administration had a particularly passive attitude to federal intervention in private commerce and state and local govern-

The 1928 National Air Races marked the opening of Mines Field, which was to become Los Angeles International Airport. The air races were a major event where new speed records were set and new technologies demonstrated.

Left: By 1930 Mines Field sported two hangars and had a runway oiled for dust control. The hangar to the right is the famous Hangar 1 owned by the Curtiss Flying Service, which still survives as a cargo office. Although the runway made it easier to find the field, the whitewash circle marking the airfield that helped pilots distinguish their destination from the surrounding fields was still in place. Mines Field is Los Angeles International Airport today.

Right: The first U.S. airline terminal designed with flair was Pan American's terminal at Miami Airport at 36th Street, opened in 1928. It was the first terminal designed by Delano and Aldrich of New York, who would go on to become one of the most respected airport architects in coming years.

ARRIVAL OF "WEST INDIES AIR LIMITED" FROM SAN JUAN & HAVANA AT PAN AMERICAN AIRWAYS AIRPORT, MIAMI.

By the late 1920s St. Louis' Lambert Field had become a busy airport, with numerous operators maintaining their own hangars, including Universal Airlines, which later became part of American Airlines. The field still lacked paved runways, but it had a wide concrete apron for aircraft parking, to make it easier for passengers on wet, muddy days.

ment, even by the standards of its time. One key administration member, however, did have faith in the future of commercial aviation and recognized the importance of an active government role in promoting it. He was Herbert Hoover, the Secretary of Commerce and a firm believer in technology and the principle of the associative state.

This principle held that the federal government's role toward the private sector and the states in economic and regulatory matters was primarily advisory. But it also recognized that as the economy was getting increasingly national, and new technologies were functioning across state lines, there was a legitimate and growing need for a modicum of government intervention on a national basis for the common good. To achieve the right balance of intervention, the federal government had to work closely with private sector trade associations, chambers of commerce, and professional associations, primarily in an advisory, coordinating role.

In Hoover's view, government officials and experts should volunteer as boosters of worthy economic and technological causes, providing comprehensive, expert advice, guidelines, and standards for the states and the private sector to use as they saw fit. But in extreme cases, carefully rationed federal regulation, funding, and even direct participation should also be forthcoming.

Hoover and his men fanned out across the country to make the case for the future of air commerce. The two pieces of aviation legislation Congress finally passed after lengthy deliberation in the mid 1920s to shape the structure of the nascent aviation industry generally reflected the principles of the associative state. For the first time, Congress confirmed that the federal government sufficiently believed in aviation's potential to provide not only advice but also legislative and even limited finan-

cial support to help it mature into a viable national commercial enterprise.

The first step was the Contract Air Mail Act of 1925, more widely known as the Kelly Act, which privatized carriage of the airmail under a bid system. As the airmail became well established and steadily expanded its reach throughout the country, it became apparent that the post office would have a difficult time running the extensive aviation operations the service required. That task was viewed as being more appropriate for private contractors whose business was flying and who would bid for the right to carry mail for government compensation on routes specified by the post office. As these routes spread, there would be a continuously growing need for airports to support them.

The Kelly Act was an important vote of confidence for the aviation industry. The government's willingness to fund the carriage of airmail encouraged investors to commit capital to starting up aviation

Universal Air Transport became American Airways in 1930. Lambert Field in St. Louis was only one of several airports that maintained a fleet of limousines to transfer passengers between the field and downtown. This practice was common at a time when personal cars were not widely owned and public transportation was a sporadic option at best.

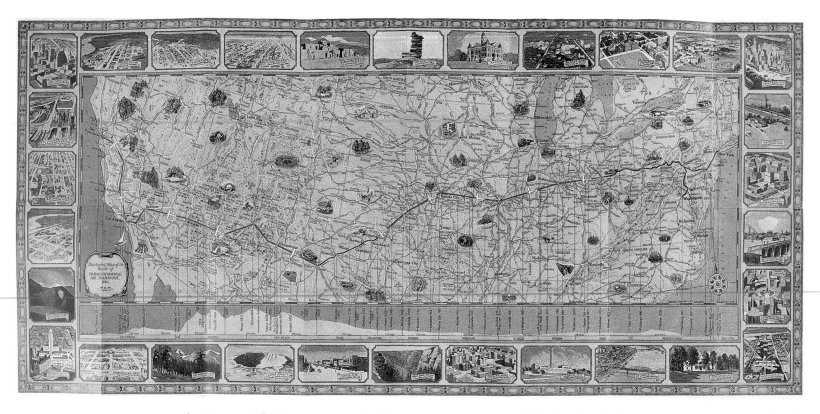

Above: Transcontinental Air Transport launched the first sustained coast-to-coast airline service in 1929 with a combined airplane/train service. Passengers rode the train by night and flew by day to shave two days off the time it took to make the trip by train. This rare map, handed out to passengers, depicts the route taken by TAT and indicates the train and plane segments.

businesses. This in turn provided hope to aviators that they might achieve some level of steady income from flying. The government also continued to encourage communities to establish airports along the new airmail routes, explaining that towns selected as stopovers could expect some level of regular air-traffic flow.

The landmark change came in 1926 with the passage of the Air Commerce Act. It was sweeping legislation that regulated for the first time the design, licensing, and operation of aircraft, set training and certification requirements for pilots, and specified standards and responsibilities for the aviation infrastructure. It also created a new federal

This ink blotter depicts passengers transferring from the train to one of TAT's Ford Trimotors on the coast-to-coast plane/train service. TAT soon became TWA.

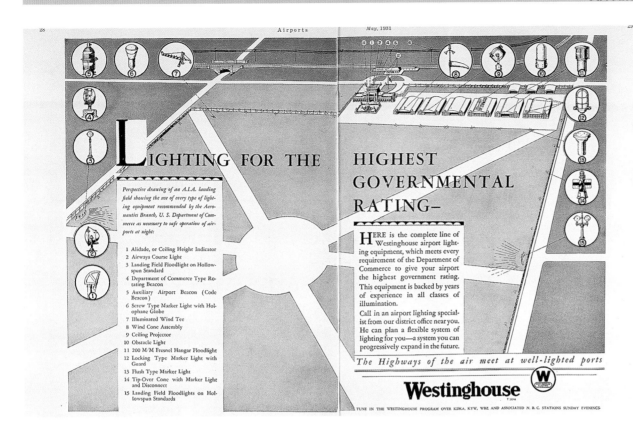

As airports proliferated and the airmail pioneered the techniques of night flying, airport lighting became an increasingly big business. Westinghouse was only one of many companies that offered a wide range of specialized lighting equipment for airports.

Below: A Northwest Airways Ford taxies up to the airline's hangar at St. Paul, Minnesota. The administrative and ticket office building is attached to the hangar, but not in the typical lean-to fashion characteristic of most hangars at the time.

bureaucracy, the Aeronautics Branch of the Commerce Department, to oversee, albeit modestly, the new industry.

The Air Commerce Act placed under federal control those aspects of the aviation industry that transcended state lines. Aircraft that operated on an interstate basis carried safety risks across state lines. Since safety was a universal concern, the design, certification, and operation of these aircraft became federal responsibilities, as did training standards and the certification of pilots who flew the aircraft.

The act also addressed responsibility for commercial aviation's operating environment: the airways and airports. It made the establishment and maintenance of airways and related navigation aids a federal responsibility, as the airway system was nationwide. With regard to airports, however, it stated that the government would not engage in constructing, owning, or operating them, nor would it finance their construction. It thus implied that airports were not a federal but a local, municipal responsibility because, in the government's view, an airport primarily benefited the local community.

This division of responsibility for airways and airports wasn't an innovation. It was similar to the manner in which the shipping industry's infrastructure was already regulated, known as the "dock" concept. The local ports had jurisdiction to build, operate, and maintain the docks, while the government was respon-

OAKLAND MUNICIPAL AIRPORT

1000 ACRES PRESENT OPERATIONS AREA
COMBINED PRESENT AND
FUTURE OPERATIONS AREA....1700 ACRES
ADDITIONAL AREA FOR AVIATION
INDUSTRIAL DEVELOPMENT.......700 ACRES
TOTAL........................2400 ACRES
PRESENT RUNWAYS AND TAXIWAYS SHOWN IN
BLACK AND WHITE

Oakland Airport rose to prominence in the public eye in late 1927 when it provided two suitably long runways to enable the contestants of the San Francisco-to-Hawaii race sponsored by Dole Pineapple Company to take off in their gasoline-laden craft. Oakland beat out San Francisco's Mills Field as the launch airport. This postcard announces further development.

sible for establishing and operating the shipping lanes and waterways. As Hoover himself explained to the *Washington Post*, "The Federal government will take the same attitude on airports as seaports. Provision for airports is the duty of municipalities, like the job of providing docks and seaports."

William P. MacCracken, a Hoover protégé appointed to run the Department of Commerce's Aeronautics Branch established under the auspices of the Air Commerce Act, was representing Hoover's view of the associative state's position regarding airports when he said, "It is the duty of every municipality to own an airport, just as much as it is its duty to own and maintain the streets, parks, and harbor facilities within its limits."

With regard to airports and airways, the Air Commerce Act codified what was already happening

nationwide. By the time it was passed, most of America's largest towns and cities had locally owned and operated airports, and the government had developed and was operating an airway system that spanned the continent. But the municipalities faced a multitude of questions and uncertainties not addressed by the legislation: Should airports be privately or municipally owned? Should a municipality own or lease its airfield? How should airport construction be financed? To what standards should airports be built? What operations and safety standards should an airport meet? These were only a handful of the broadest questions to which local and state governments sought answers.

The associative state had at least some of the answers and was ready to provide them in a voluntary, advisory capacity, primarily through staff consultation

TRUSCON STEEL HANGARS AND STEEL HANGAR DOORS

TANNER AIRPLANE HANGAR, Santa Monica, California
Truscon Airplane Hangar Doors (Straight Slide Type)

STANDARD OIL COMPANY HANGAR, Memphis, Tenn.
Truscon Steel Hangar with Airplane Hangar Doors

WRIGHT FIELD ASSEMBLY BUILDING
Green County, Ohio
Truscon Airplane Hangar Doors
(Straight Slide Type)

NATIONAL AIR TRANSPORT, Inc.,
Chicago, Ill.
Truscon Airplane Hangar Doors
(Curved Track Type)

NATIONAL AIR TRANSPORT, Inc.,
Chicago, Ill.
Truscon Airplane Hangar Doors
(Curved Track Type)

STANDARD OIL HANGAR, Chicago, Ill.
Truscon Airplane Hangar Doors (Curved Track Type)

LE ROY HANGAR,
Rochester, N. Y.
Truscon Airplane Hangar Doors
(Curved Track Type)

CURTISS FLYING SERVICE HANGAR, Louisville, Ky
Truscon Airplane Hangar Doors (Curved Track Type)

METAL AIRCRAFT CORPORATION, Cincinnati, Ohio
Truscon Steel Hangar with Airplane Hangar Doors

LANSDOWNE HANGAR, Youngstown, Ohio
Truscon Steel Hangar with Airplane Hangar Doors

and a series of periodicals, circulars, and bulletins issued by the Commerce Department's Aeronautics Branch. These publications included periodic news letters, statistical information, and, most importantly for would-be airport operators, a steady stream of manuals on airport design, construction, and operation.

Although social enthusiasm for aviation was relatively high by 1926, there wasn't a municipal stampede to build airports following passage of the Air Commerce Act. One limitation was practical. Because responsibility for airports was relegated to local authorities, the individual state and local governments had to pass their own enabling legislation to authorize municipalities to raise public financing for airport construction. A handful of farsighted states, including Indiana, Kansas, Nebraska, Wisconsin, and Pennsylvania, had approved such legislation prior to 1926, but most states had not, and they faced a long, messy process of working through the legal options and challenges.

The rapid development of public airports faced another, more human constraint. Fervent believers in aviation readily embraced what historian Joseph Corn called the "Winged Gospel." It was a theological conviction that the conquest of the air was humankind's ultimate technological triumph, and the better life it promised for all was just a matter of time. But believers were still relatively few in numbers at that time.

The broader population, though increasingly fascinated by flight, continued to see little chance of ever personally benefiting from the airplane. Even the airmail, the most visible practical application of aviation, was much too expensive a means for the

The Truscon Company's brochure reveals its varied line of hangars. Each example is a real hangar already completed. Note the many communities that had airports by the late 1920s.

A flight of army MB-2 bombers in formation from nearby Mitchell Field wheels over Roosevelt Field on Long Island. Airports dotted Long Island before World War II with its close proximity to Manhattan, but most fell victim to developers in the postwar boom.

Below: The passengers of Pan American's Fokker Trimotors walked out to their aircraft under a shaded awning at the airline's Miami terminal. It provided some relief from the rain and the sun, but on hot summer days passengers suffered until the aircraft climbed to altitude and benefited from natural air conditioning.

Airports and Airlines

December
1931

IN THIS ISSUE
Air Transport Operations In Latin America
By Charles L. Lawrance

average person to send correspondence. Immobile and ignorant of air transport advances in Europe, most Americans still saw the airplane as a dangerous, fragile, unreliable, expensive, and marginally practical machine—entertainment and adventure craft, not transportation. So when they were asked to vote large sums of their own money for municipal bonds to finance airport construction, they were understandably reluctant.

American aviation badly needed a hero, a super celebrity whose symbol could effectively convey to the masses the substance the boosters so fervently believed. On May 20, 1927, it got one. He was Charles Lindbergh, an introspective, lanky, ex-airmail pilot who flew nonstop from New York to Paris in 33 and a half hours in the *Spirit of St. Louis*, his custombuilt, single-engined Ryan monoplane, and became the best known pilot for the rest of the 20th century.

As news of Lindbergh's triumph flashed through the news wires, millions embraced the Winged Gospel overnight. Here, at last, was spectacular symbolic confirmation of the airplane's promise. The wings of commerce and industry were now sure to follow, and woe to the community that had no airport to embrace the coming air age.

Municipal councils, chambers of commerce, and local business associations everywhere agitated for airport construction. The Guggenheim Fund to further air transportation was established. Many municipalities could count on an appearance from Lindbergh as he roamed the nation with the *Spirit of St. Louis* on a 22,000-mile, three-month publicity tour upon his return to the United States. When he managed to break loose from the crowds that could number over 100,000, he frequently bumped into other aviation worthies circulating among local communities of all sizes at the behest of the Department of Commerce's Aeronautics Branch, exhorting the public to build airports.

In the aftermath of Lindbergh's flight, a flurry of legislative activity swept though state and local governments to address the perceived needs of commercial aviation. Over the next three years, 33 states passed some form of enabling legislation authorizing the funding, construction, and operation of public airports.

Private airfields still significantly outnumbered public airports at this time, and a debate ensued about the desirability of relying on them to meet public needs. The Curtiss Corporation was particularly aggressive in expanding its privately owned network of airports around the nation. Hoping to balance the public interest against this growth in privatization, most states and municipalities, as well as the federal government, favored the public ownership of airports officially designated to serve their communities.

Airport construction gathered steam as a result of these developments. Aggressive private-sector concerns like Pan American, TAT, and the Curtiss companies continued to build private airports at strategic spots to serve their specific needs. But publicly owned airports quickly gained ground and matched those in private hands available for public use.

In the absence of standard legislative requirements, airport ownership and financing structures varied from community to community to suit local circumstances. Many municipalities encountered

Hadley Field in New Jersey was the official airmail stop for New York for years, even after the opening of Newark Airport closer to the city, because it had the best weather in the metropolitan area. The airmail moved to Newark after improvements in flying in instrument conditions.

The Douglas M-2 mail plane was one of Donald Douglas' first successful creations, long before the DC-3. It carried the mail on the routes of Western Air Express from California as far as Salt Lake City, Utah.

to locate its airport, leasing a site was often a viable interim alternative to buying one. This was the solution of aviation boosters in Los Angeles, who had the municipality lease Mines Field in 1928. Today the field is Los Angeles International Airport.

The role of boosters to convert the local community to the cause of building an airport was all important. Boosters could be enlightened members of municipal government or local civic organizations such as the chamber of commerce, local chapters of the Lions Club, Rotary Club, and similar organizations, and even women's civic associations.

In Atlanta the Chamber of Commerce, the Junior Chamber of Commerce, the Atlanta Woman's Club, the Better Films Committee, the American Legion, and the Greater Atlanta Club all clamored for an airfield. They secured an offer from Asa Candler, founder of Coca-Cola, to lease the Candler Field speedway on concessionary terms with an option to buy. Their efforts paid off. In 1925 the city council voted to accept Candler's offer. The boosters had an ally in city government, a young alderman who would eventually wind up as Atlanta's Mayor. His name was William B. Hartsfield. Candler Field is Atlanta Hartsfield Airport today.

In several cases, where widespread booster enthusiasm was backed by financial resources, the booster groups took matters into their own hands and funded the creation of an airport for municipal use. This was the case in Dayton, Ohio, and Muncie, Indiana.

Once the decision to build an airport was approved and financing secured, a community or private company faced a daunting technical task. There was little precedent for guidance in the new, rapidly evolving business of aviation. Its conventions and standards were being created concurrently with its infrastructure.

It was becoming obvious that a commercial airport was only one vital link in a radically new and complex transportation system. A commercial airport could not be viewed in a vacuum if it were to become a commercial success. Its creation required a wide array of interdisciplinary skills, including civil engineering, architecture, urban

little resistance from the local community to acquiring or designating land for the establishment of an airport and issuing bonds to finance its construction. In some instances, designated land was already in municipal hands. In others it could be acquired on relatively favorable terms from a private believer in the Winged Gospel. In some instances a state chose to build its own chain of airports in addition to municipal and private initiatives.

Where a municipality encountered resistance to an airport initiative or was uncertain about where

planning (itself a relatively new field), and financial planning and management. Professionals in these disciplines had little or no experience creating airports, so they faced a steep learning curve in an exponentially changing industry where projecting future trends and needs was particularly difficult. In addition, these various professions weren't particularly good at cooperating with each other.

Initially, the construction of airports was seen primarily as a task for civil engineering. Following guidance from the aviation community with regard to field size, orientation, and location, the civil engineers' main job was the preparation of the field surface. The objective was to provide a well-graded surface usable year round, with excellent drainage to effectively handle wet weather—a significant challenge considering the day's standard soft-surface runways.

Above: Opening day for the municipal hangar at Mines Field in Los Angeles in 1930. A big air rally is in progress as the airplane is becoming the favorite possession of the enthusiastic sportsman pilot. The building survives today at Los Angeles International Airport as a cargo office.

This typical lean-to terminal of the early 1930s, at the Curtiss hangar in Memphis, Tennessee, was modeled on a factory assembly building with attached administrative offices.

Below: National Parks Airways operated from airports along some of the most forbidding terrain in the United States, connecting Salt Lake City with Great Falls, Montana. Navigation was quite simple along a north-south line paralleling a prominent ridge line, but the weather could be a formidable obstacle, especially in winter.

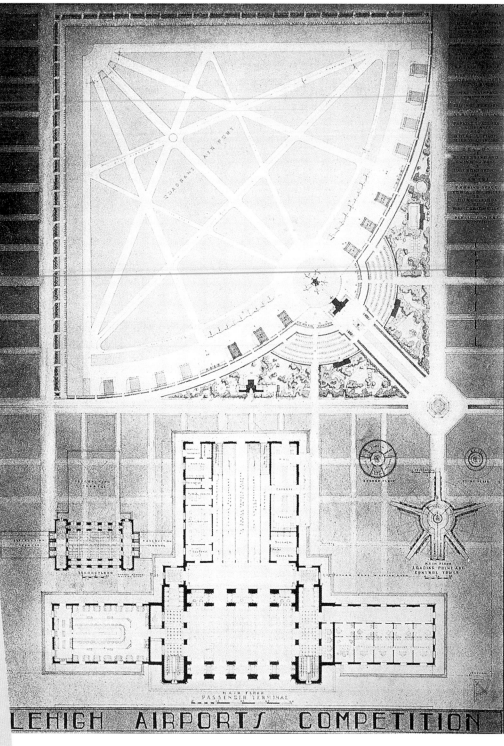

Above: The Leigh Portland Cement Airport Competition of 1929 was primarily an attempt to sell more cement, but it drew many of the time's best architects, and the entries presented novel features that have since become common at airports. Note the winning bid's circular satellite terminal design for aircraft boarding.

Soft surface preparation was a complex task with many options for choice of turf. A poor soft-surface job eventually resulted in clouds of dust in dry weather and axle-deep mud when it rained. It is instructive to read some of the turf recommendations in one of the Aeronautics Branch's early Airport Design and Construction bulletins.

In the northern half of the country the report generally recommended 80 percent Kentucky bluegrass and 20 percent redtop. In the Northeast the redtop could be increased, and in the more acid soils of New England a bentgrass-redtop mixture was said to work best. Pure bluegrass was the choice in the Mid-Atlantic states, and timothy should be added in humid northern regions. Bermuda grass worked best in the Southeast, sown at 25-30 pounds per acre for quickest results (compared to 100-150 pounds per acre of bluegrass further north). Broomegrass or crested wheatgrass was the turf of choice in the northern Great Plains where rainfall is moderate.

This map by the Curtiss Flying Company shows the proliferation of airports throughout the country by the early 1930s. Note the number of major airports highlighted in the New York area.

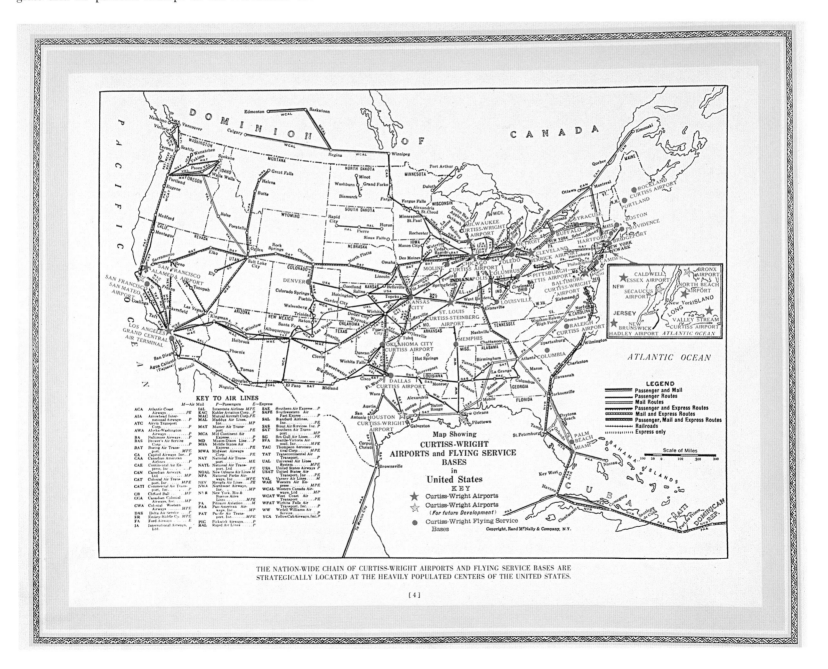

THE NATION-WIDE CHAIN OF CURTISS-WRIGHT AIRPORTS AND FLYING SERVICE BASES ARE STRATEGICALLY LOCATED AT THE HEAVILY POPULATED CENTERS OF THE UNITED STATES.

[4]

STANDARD AIR LINES

The FAIR WEATHER ROUTE

LOS ANGELES - PHOENIX
TUCSON - DOUGLAS AND
EL PASO

Left: Standard Airlines offers Fokker service to airports in southern California and the southwest. The fair weather route is not mentioned to attract tourists but to reassure frightened passengers.

Above: This modest float plane and amphibian jetty at North Beach on Bowery Bay was the beginning of New York's LaGuardia Airport.

Above: At Chicago's Sky Harbor Airport a hangar with a decorative Art Deco concrete façade projects a modern look. While attractive, such treatments were expensive for a functional building serving a financially strapped industry.

The bulletin also warned that while turf runways had been the longtime standard, they did not stand up well to heavy use, as seen recently with the rapidly increasing air traffic at certain airports. It noted that for the busiest airports, a need for hard-surface runways might well be inevitable, but it did not provide a broad endorsement of hard-surface runways, because they were extremely expensive. Instead, the bulletin pointed out that highway engineers had devised low-cost alternatives to the paved highway on secondary roads, but cautioned that some techniques might not work ideally because they relied on continuous vehicle traffic for ultimate compaction. Loose stones, a minor problem for automobiles, could also be a major hazard for wooden propellers.

The soft-surface/hard-surface runway debate was heating up in the nascent airport construction community by the late 1920s. As traffic volumes increased and airplanes were becoming larger and heavier, it was clear that for most commercial uses the days of the turf runway were numbered. In 1929, the Ford Airplane Company, maker of the Ford Trimotor, one of the heaviest transports of the day, boldly paved a 2,500-foot runway at its Dearborn, Michigan, airport, creating the first truly hard-surface runway in the United States. Ford liked the results so much that the following year it paved another runway to handle different wind conditions.

There should have been little debate about the preference for all-weather paved runways, but oddly enough there wasn't unanimous enthusiasm. Many airports didn't have the money to build them. Pilots preferred the softer landings on grass that made them look good. And some engineers worried about the undue stress the landing gear could suffer from touching down on concrete. Hard-surface advocates suggested that it was perhaps time for the tail skid to go in favor of the tail wheel. But in spite of such reservations, by 1930 the concrete runway had made its appearance at the busiest airports and in the next decade it steadily gained ground at most airports providing regular commercial service.

While airport surface preparation ideally required open-minded highway engineers with a keen interest in their lawns, the art of drainage was more uniformly transferable from other civil engineering applications. It was a critical task because wet weather could shut down an airport for

Washington, D.C. didn't have an airport worthy of the capital for many years, but it did provide joy rides for sightseers. A flight typically lasted 15 minutes and covered all the monuments in a sweeping circle.

FLY OVER WASHINGTON

WASHINGTON-HOOVER AIRPORT

Above: United Airlines' downtown ticketing office in San Francisco. The limousine is on standby, awaiting passengers. Airline offices became prestigious places that did their best to attract dreamers and doers to the brave new way to travel.

Right: The 150-mile route of the Salt Lake City to Pocatello, Idaho, segment of National Parks Airways' route system was illustrated in a company brochure given to passengers to allow them more easily to follow the flight path and identify the sights below. Note the lighted beacons which are all on emergency landing fields.

days, bringing significant revenue losses, and landing on a waterlogged soft runway could be spectacularly dangerous.

Another important civil engineering task was the marking of the airport environment, including the runways, boundaries, and nearby obstructions. Landing direction markers or wind tees were also required, and windsocks had to be placed in the right spots. Airports also had their names painted in large letters in a prominent location, usually a hangar roof. Prompted by the night-flying experience of the Air Mail, many airports also installed night lighting, which was developing into a sub-specialty of the aviation industry. Lighting included flood lights, boundary lights, airport beacons visible from a distance to help pilots find the airport, lit wind socks and wind tees, and the lighting of the letters spelling out the airport's name.

Most early airport builders had a utilitarian attitude to airport buildings. The government's *Airport Design and Construction* bulletin's discourse on grasses and airport beacons was longer than its section on airport buildings. The most important structure was the airport hangar, the design and construction of which

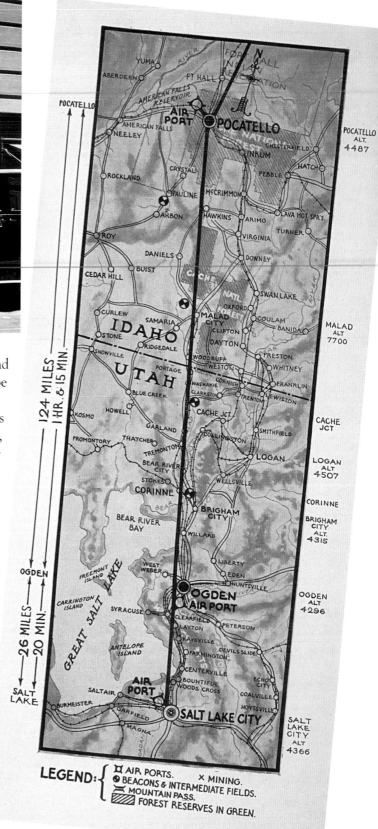

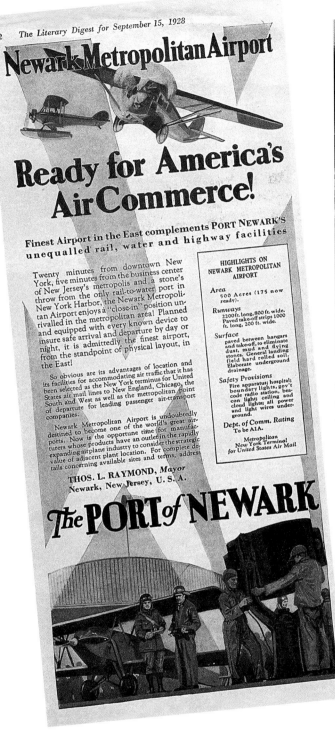

The opening of Newark Airport in 1928 was a clever coup to capture for the New Jersey town the title of being the airport that served New York. Newark maintained its hold on the New York traffic until the construction of LaGuardia, and today it is once again the busiest airport in the metropolitan New York area, Handling over 25 million passengers a year.

usually fell to the civil engineer. The construction techniques of large-span, open-space structures in both wood and steel were well understood from the experience of building railroad sheds, factory buildings, and other industrial structures.

Administrative buildings and passenger terminals tended to get minimal attention. A common solution was to attach the administrative building to the hangar's side in lean-to fashion, a practice borrowed from the building structures that inspired the hangars. The services offered in the administrative building depended on the airport's size and traffic volume. Ideally, it included a modest passenger hall and ticketing area, an airport manager's office, a weather office, communications office, baggage area, and a modest restaurant or coffee shop.

Advice continued to flow from the government. Building on the circulars issued by the U.S. Army Air Service, the Aeronautics Branch began a comprehensive effort to develop recommended standards for airports. A helpful starting point for entities planning to develop an airport was the voluntary ratings system the Aeronautics Branch established, which was the first effort to standardize airport types.

The Rahway, New Jersey, airway direction marker. It lit up at night. Such markers were indispensable to finding the way in aviation's early days. They live on in the airport names printed on the tarmac in bold yellow letters at the smaller, primarily recreational airports.

An Airplane In Every Garage

Eugene Vidal, appointed to head the Bureau of Air Commerce in 1932, was typical of the many aviation boosters of his time, obsessed with visions of an America with an airplane in every garage. Their dream proved to be utopian, but for some it has come true. There are over 450 airports in the United States where the taxiways lead to hangars that look like oversized garages attached to private homes. They are private fly-in communities whose residents' associations own the airfield and whose inhabitants park their airplanes next to the family car.

Fly-in communities range from modest grass strips with a few houses scattered around the field to major estates with multimillion-dollar homes and a runway capable of handling private jetliners. They are found throughout the country with the highest concentrations in Florida, Washington state, and Texas.

They tend to attract two types of residents: those whose lives revolve around their extreme interest in flying, and those whose lifestyles require them to frequently use private airplanes to reach destinations nationwide. A home in a fly-in community and a capable airplane can make possible ambitious business travel schedules that could never be accomplished on scheduled airlines.

One of the earliest and most well established fly-in communities is Spruce Creek, near Daytona Beach, Florida. It used to be Samsula Field, a World War II-era surplus military airport, until it was acquired by investors in 1970 to be transformed into the Spruce Creek fly-in community.

Today Spruce Creek spreads across 1,200 acres ringing its 4,000-foot paved, lit runway. It has 1,600 homes ranging from condominiums accessible by the average well-off family to mansions costing several million dollars. There are 12 distinct neighborhoods within Spruce Creek, each with its own architectural style and atmosphere. The majority of the houses have their own attached hangars, and there is also communal hangar space

The Cessna 120 in this late-1940s image advertises the dream of an airplane in every garage in the aftermath of World War II. Certain boosters had hopes of turning the massive wartime capacity for aircraft production into a peace dividend.

The rating system had three components. A letter code ranked airports from "A" to "D" based on the extent of their facilities and services. "A" was the highest ranking, awarded to airports with the most extensive facilities for passengers, a weather office, communications capabilities, and comprehensive aircraft servicing and repair facilities.

The second component was a numerical code, ranking airports from 1 to 4 by available landing area. To earn a 1, the highest rating, an airport had to have at least 2,500 feet available for landing or takeoff in all directions. If this was impractical, the alternative standard was a minimum of four runways that were at least 2,500 feet long and 500 feet wide, allowing take-offs and landings in eight directions and providing an option for all wind conditions. Airports rated 4 needed only 1,300 feet for takeoffs and landings in all directions, or two runways at least 1,800 feet long and 500 feet wide facing prevailing winds.

The last component was another letter code that ranged from A to E to cover airports that provided regular lighting facilities. A rating of X

and tiedowns. A country club and 18-hole golf course provide distractions for those weary of flying.

Spruce Creek attracts a wide cross-section of residents. Entrepreneurs and professional race car drivers jet around the country from their doorsteps. Others work closer to home and are joined by their love of recreational flying. The community also has its share of airline pilots who commute to work in their own planes, and retirees who spend more time in their hangars and planes than in their living rooms.

The airplanes are as varied as the residents. They range from the most exquisitely restored antique biplanes through ordinary single- and twin-engined piston airplanes to turboprops and business jets. There are also exotic warbirds, aerobatic airplanes, and motorgliders.

Across the country in Eatonville, Washington, is Swanson Field, a 3,000-foot strip ringed by the homes of nine flying families. They are an informal lot, including a longshoreman, loggers, and a couple of retired airline pilots. They don't get hung up on formality. Everyone pitches in to mow the grass to keep the maintenance costs down.

By the 1980s the dream had become reality, but only for some. A Raytheon Beech Baron is parked next to its owner's house at the Spruce Creek, Florida, fly-in community.

Back in Florida, at Jumbolair Aviation Estates near Ocala, mowing their own grass is farthest from the residents' mind. The 550-acre estate was once home to a Vanderbilt heiress, thousands of crocodiles, 98 African elephants, a couple of rhinos, and a 400-pound gorilla called Mickey. In 2002 it was being converted into America's most luxurious fly-in community by its owner, Terri Thayer, former Revlon model and a Boeing 747-rated pilot.

Jumbolair's main attraction is its 7,550-foot runway, which makes it the only fly-in community capable of accepting jet airliners. Thayer hopes that this will prove irresistible to the handful of private airplane owners who fly converted jetliners and want to park them next to their houses. First among them to opt for one of Jumbolair's 125 home sites was actor and experienced jet pilot John Travolta, who flies as much as 350 hours a year in his ex-Quantas Boeing 707. That's quite an airplane to put in his garage.

applied to airports with no lighting at all or lighting not regularly available.

This rating system, launched in 1929, was voluntary. An airport wishing to be rated could request an inspection from the Department of Commerce. The first airport to be rated was the municipal airport of Pontiac, Michigan, which received an A1A rating in 1930. Besides giving the airport community some sense of standards of which to aspire, the rating system's value was primarily in marketing. The phrase "A1A rated," or, more commonly, "built to A1A standards," began to show up in the advertising material of a handful of the largest commercial airports to reassure passengers that the highest level of service and safety was available.

Airport builders could also turn to the Aeronautics Branch for airport marking and lighting standards. In addition, that organization circulated basic information on airport design and construction in a variety of publications, backed up by expert staff. It also distributed suggested operating rules and standards that most airports adopted.

Detroit Airport's hangar had an impressive series of doors that opened up the entire length of the building to the parking apron. The hangar could also be compartmentalized for multiple clients. The method of building such large-span structures was well understood from erecting factory buildings to house, among other things, townie Henry Ford's assembly lines.

Below: The National Air Races moved around from site to site, but Cleveland came to be thought of as the national center for air racing because the Nationals were so frequently held there. It was a great venue for Jimmy Doolittle, Roscoe Turner, Matty Laird, and others. Today it lives on as Cleveland Hopkins Airport.

The circulars also addressed a dilemma faced by airport planners of the day. The land-based, fixed-wing airplane wasn't the only aircraft that required landing fields. Where suitable bodies of water existed, seaplanes were more practical and just as capable as the landplanes. On long, over-water legs, seaplanes were considered safer, having a significantly greater chance of making a successful emergency landing.

Seaplanes were correctly seen as having an increasingly important role in overseas and coastal operations. The amphibian, a hybrid of the seaplane and landplane, which could use both seaports and airports, seemed to have a particularly promising future. Thus, the seaplane base was as important a concern for the commercial aviation industry as the airport, and was covered in some detail by various advisory circulars.

Another aircraft providing great utility and even greater promise as a global means of air travel was the airship. Dirigibles were proving to be effective patrol craft for the military, offering very long range and the ability to remain aloft for days. And in 1928 the German airship *Graf Zeppelin* dramatically launched the era of long-distance commercial airship travel with a perfect round-the-world flight. In the United States, where the airship industry was less advanced than in Germany, airship operations remained within the sphere of the military, which created airship bases featuring enormous dirigible hangars.

As the demand for airports grew, the emerging airport development community began to generate its own sources of information and support organizations. Several engineers published works addressing airport construction, and in 1929 the first airport conference was organized in Cleveland, Ohio, attended by over 200 participants from throughout the nation.

Companies began to specialize in airport-specific products and services. Standard hangar models were offered by several companies nationwide with experience in building factories and other large open-span structures. Lighting companies began to develop and produce comprehensive lines of aviation-specific lighting products. Fuel suppliers set up aviation divisions. The development and production of aviation-specific meteorological instruments

Airport weather information became critically important for safety as aviation progressed and aircraft operators carrying paying passengers were increasingly willing to tackle challenging weather. The airport weather observers collected local data, including cloud ceiling height, wind, visibility, temperature, air pressure, and humidity, and radioed it to other airports and inbound aircraft.

and communications equipment accelerated. And multidisciplinary engineering firms began to specialize in airport design and construction. Several of them, including the Austin Company, are still in business.

With a handful of exceptions, architects were largely absent from the field of airport development. The airport continued to be seen mostly as an engineering problem, a viewpoint jealously guarded by the engineering community. Air terminals were expensive and, in the view of practical engineers who cared little for marketing and customer service, added little value to an airport. Most terminals were a lean-to added on to the side of a hangar which drew its architectural and engineering inspiration from factory buildings and railroad sheds. But as air traffic grew, that approach was about to change.

Budding airline executives, aviation journalists on air travel assignments, Aeronautics Branch experts, and the steadily increasing number of

Floyd Bennett Field in Brooklyn, New York, was opened with great fanfare in 1931 as an alternative to thriving Newark, but it was too far from Manhattan to take away from its rival the all-important airmail terminus designation, and was shunned by the major airlines. Later it became an important Naval Air Station for many years.

airline passengers all began to realize that the passenger's needs were poorly catered to at most airports. Wealthy travelers used to opulent surrounding, servants, and chauffeurs were not amused by airport waiting rooms one step up from a woodshed. Nor would that image win over droves of converts to going by air.

The dearth of architecturally designed airport terminals at a time when America was falling in love with reinforced concrete also came to the attention of the Leigh Portland Cement Company. This aggressive firm correctly foresaw in aviation a chance to sell billions of tons of cement in coming years and decided to jumpstart their marketing opportunity by

announcing the Leigh Airports Competition of 1928, a design competition to create the ideal municipal airport. Recognizing the hitherto neglected importance of the passenger terminal, the organizers especially welcomed participation by architects.

The competition offered $10,000 in prizes and was judged by an interdisciplinary panel that recognized the eclectic nature of airport planning and design. The judges were independent of the Leigh Portland Cement Company and represented the disciplines of architecture, civil engineering, aeronautics, and civics and urban planning. Among them were the dean of the Columbia School of Architecture, the editor of *Architectural Forum*, the publishing director of *Engineering News Record*, and the president of the Curtiss Flying Service.

The design criteria specified that entrants present a comprehensive municipal airport plan that included requirements for the secure separation of airside and landside functions, parking for automobiles, access by mass transit as well as an airport highway, and integration with the served city's urban plan. It also assigned prime importance to the passenger terminal among the buildings at the airport.

Superbly publicized, the Leigh Airports Competition turned into the landmark event that firmly established the role of the airport architect alongside the airport civil engineer.

The results demonstrated the ability of some of the country's most talented architects to create groundbreaking design concepts for an industry with little precedent. It also showed the difficulty of foreseeing the future needs of an industry that was evolving rapidly in directions unclear even to its most visionary participants.

The Leigh Airports Competition's designs confidently affirmed that the airport was to be seen not as a local facility but as an integral link between the community it serves and the national transportation grid. It showcased the importance of efficient, well-planned road and rail connections to the city. It also affirmed that the hard-surface, all-weather runways and accompanying taxiways were to be the new standard for commercial airports.

On the airport's airside, where the air operations were conducted, several of the designs foretold features that were ahead of their time and would be adopted in some variation later as air transportation grew in coming years. Most notable was the recognition by several participants of the advantage of parallel runways for increasing air traffic capacity. The linear row of boarding gates easily expandable at either end, and the star cluster and finger layout of boarding gates, all made their appearance in some fashion.

One entry, which merited only honorable mention in the judges' view, presented for the first time the concept of separating arriving and departing passengers by upper and lower floors to maximize passenger flow. That design would first be

employed at LaGuardia Airport a decade later and has since become a global standard.

Another innovation, evident in several designs, was a forerunner of the enclosed telescopic boarding tunnel that much later became another standard airport feature worldwide, commonly known as the "jetway." Today the jetway protects us from the elements and speeds up boarding and disembarkation. It also has a safety benefit, keeping us shielded from the airport ramp, which was the competition participant's primary inspiration. The main concern of that designer was protecting passengers from whirling propellers, as it was a standard practice at the time to have the engines running and warmed up for a quick departure after boarding.

The emphasis placed by the competition on passenger terminals produced splendid Art Deco designs. These were far more opulent and passenger-oriented than any existing terminal, but mimicked in a fairly conservative fashion the more elegant railroad stations of the time.

One shortcoming of the competition's airport designs was that practically all of them would have been obsolete by the time they could have been built.

United Airlines' ticket office in downtown San Francisco caters to its well-heeled clientele in the 1930s. Travel agents also sold airline tickets, but many people preferred to go in person to the airline offices to make their travel arrangements.

The Grand Central Air Terminal in Glendale, California, was one of the most important airports serving Los Angeles. It was TWA's and American Airways' western base and a popular general aviation airport. United flew from its own company-owned airport in nearby Burbank.

Below: This hangar at Pontiac, Michigan, the nation's first A1A-rated airport, is lit for night operations and maintenance. Driven by the aggressive airmail culture, commercial aviation was a 24-hour operation from the earliest days.

Contestants couldn't foresee the dramatic growth in aircraft performance and passenger capacity. The sleek new airliners would need more room to operate comfortably than the space provided for by the proposed airports. Notably, most designs provided little scope for significantly expanding the airport area and runway space.

Another drawback was that the designs, especially for the terminals, were too costly for real-world application, given the low traffic volumes at the time and the consequent precarious financial condition of commercial aviation. The announcement of the competition's results less than a month after the stock market crash of 1929 and the onset of the Great Depression further dampened the chances of rapid implementation of the best designs.

In spite of these limitations, the Leigh Airports Competition effectively presented the broad topics and principles the interdisciplinary airport design and

East Boston Airport in the 1930s was a thriving center of aviation. A Ford Trimotor airliner of Colonial Airways takes off on another run to New York, while private flyers line the apron. Owning an airplane was a status symbol for the rich, conveying a daring, progressive image. But it wasn't all social posturing; it was also a great way to cut down the commute to their favorite out-of-town haunts, many of which were on islands.

construction industry needed to consider and was a catalyst for debate within the industry which is still ongoing and is a key stimulant to professional progress.

The government also weighed in with a standard design of a simple terminal that could be adapted to local needs. And in the real world, under the leadership of a few farsighted architects, the passenger-friendly airport terminal design was slowly beginning to make progress.

A handful of designs even preceded the Leigh Airports Competition by a year or two. These progressive terminals were mostly built from private resources, free from the constraints of municipal financing. More modest in aspiration than the competition entries but a long way beyond the lean-to terminal, they would also provide valuable inspiration in coming years.

One of the first modern American air terminals was designed and built by Albert Kahn, the Detroit-based industrial architect who designed the generic Air Corps training field of World War I. He was commissioned by Henry Ford to design a terminal for the well-publicized airport Ford had established for his airmail operations and the production of the Ford Trimotor at Dearborn, Michigan, just outside Detroit.

Completed in 1928 the small, boxy, two-story stand-alone building had the austere lines of Kahn's modern, functional factory buildings. A hint of stylized Art Deco columns embedded in the façade provided minimal ornamentation. The lower story contained a simple waiting room, offices, and modest but essential amenities. The upper, smaller story was suitable for monitoring airport activity. Windows wrapped around both stories provided a flood of natural light, increasing the sense of space inside.

The Ford terminal was an early example of a simple terminal, well suited for comfortable, no-

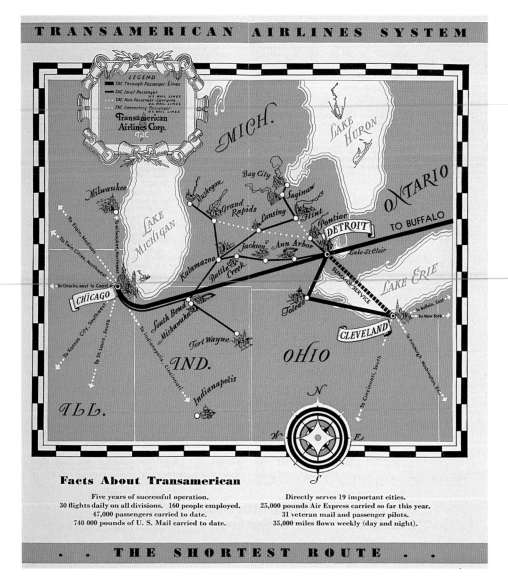

TRANSAMERICAN AIRLINES SYSTEM

LEGEND
TAC Through Passenger Lines
TAC local Passenger
U.S. MAIL LINES
TAC Non-Passenger-Carrying
U.S. MAIL LINES
TAC Connecting Passenger
U.S. MAIL LINES

Transamerican
Airlines Corp.
TAC

Facts About Transamerican

Five years of successful operation.	Directly serves 19 important cities.
30 flights daily on all divisions. 160 people employed.	25,000 pounds Air Express carried so far this year.
47,000 passengers carried to date.	31 veteran mail and passenger pilots.
740 000 pounds of U. S. Mail carried to date.	35,000 miles flown weekly (day and night).

. . THE SHORTEST ROUTE . .

By the early 1930s many local airlines provided extensive regional service, about which little is known today. Transamerican Airlines connected the Great Lakes area's big industrial centers, operating 30 flights a day. Note the proliferation of airfields along its routes. Transamerican Airlines was one of many regional lines that were merged into American Airlines.

nonsense airport operations. Its design could be varied to accommodate different volumes of passenger traffic, and it would satisfy passengers without making a disproportionate claim on the airport's financial resources. When Henry Ford had two runways paved during the following two years, he had what he could justifiably call a model airport.

Meanwhile, far from Dearborn's frigid winters, in the balmy tropical breezes of Florida a young airline entrepreneur was plotting a global airline empire that would bring him sufficient fame to rival Henry Ford's name recognition for a time. He was Juan Trippe, founder and chairman of Pan American Airways System, and by 1928 he needed a much

larger and more stylish airline terminal than the Ford terminal to make a statement about his aspirations. He hired the New York firm of Delano and Aldrich to design and build it at Pan American's Miami terminus, launching the architectural firm on a long, distinguished career of airport construction.

Delano and Aldrich's Pan American Airways terminal at Miami Airport was a graceful reinforced concrete structure, inspired in part by a traditional hangar shape and in part by a railroad station. Its interior housed a vast, airy waiting hall with check-in and ticketing counters along the sides and offices on a second floor ringing the central two-story space. On the second floor, looking out onto the boarding area, was a crescent-shaped dining terrace, first of the elegant airport restaurants that would soon to be an indispensable feature of the more important commercial airports.

Passengers came out of the terminal along a wide, covered corridor to board their departing flights, which had room to taxi up to the terminal two at a time. It is interesting to note that even a man of such maniacal aviation aspirations as Juan Trippe did not see the need at the time for being able to board more than two aircraft at any one time directly from the terminal.

Another notable early airline terminal was the Transcontinental Air Transport terminal at Port Columbus, Ohio, completed in time for TAT's launch of its transcontinental air/rail service in July, 1929. Passengers departed New York's Grand Central Station the night before on a luxury train to Port Columbus. Arriving in the morning, they boarded a TAT trimotor and flew all day to Waynoka, Oklahoma, for another night train to Clovis, New Mexico. There they embarked on another trimotor for the last leg, and reached Los Angeles, California, 48 hours after they left New York if all went well.

TAT spared no expense to set up its chain of airports across the country, relying on a mix of municipal airports and their own facilities to provide passengers as safe and high a standard of service as was possible at the time. Airport and equipment selection and the establishment of the route were personally supervised by Charles Lindbergh. Lindbergh's association with TAT allowed the airline to

In the 1930s East Boston Airport also catered to flying boats, as important a long-range aircraft as the landplanes, especially in overwater international operations. This Junkers float plane flew mail from the transatlantic ocean liner *Bremen*. It had flown out to the *Bremen* from Germany with a load of mail after the ship had departed, piggybacked on the liner across mid-ocean, and when it was within range of Boston it was launched, saving three days on the transatlantic mail service. Here it prepares to fly out to the *Bremen* on its way back to Germany.

call itself the Lindbergh Line, a slogan it continued to use long after it became TWA.

The Port Columbus terminal was a large, rectangular, Art Deco building, the most elaborate on TAT's transcontinental route. It had a fancy hexagonal tower structure at one end with a tower cab that resembled a glass cage. It was a combination railroad station/airport terminal. Passengers disembarked from the train on one side and strolled across to board the airplane on the other side.

Port Columbus was built at TAT's behest, and the airline contributed to the cost of the terminal's construction, but the airport was municipal, financed by an $850,000 bond issue in 1928 that took several efforts to raise. Designed to the highest A1A specifications, it was large by the government's recommended standards, covering 534 acres, and had two paved runways. Three large hangars were built in a style matching the terminal. They were occupied by TAT, the Curtiss Flying Service, and the municipality.

By 1928 Hilo Airport was one of several airports in Hawaii. The islands were a natural environment for the airplane, which could connect them at over ten times the speed of the fastest inter-island boats.

Burbank Airport on opening day. It was built and owned by United Airlines, then the transport arm of Boeing. Note the airport marker circle on the runway. The airport was later bought by Lockheed, which built its main plant on the open field behind the terminal. The terminal still exists but has been greatly altered.

Ford Airport, Pan American's Miami base, Port Columbus, and an increasing number of other airports were taking the initiative to set new standards for the growing commercial aviation industry. In the wake of the Air Commerce Act and the Lindbergh craze, the number of airports soared nationwide. In 1925 there were about 600 airports. By 1932 there were over 2,000.

But the results were mixed at best. Many municipalities lacked the funds and the expertise to properly build an airport. They allocated too little land. They skimped on essential but invisible requirements such as proper drainage. They saved on surfacing and lighting. And they couldn't provide the services expected at an airport, such as fuel and mechanics. Consequently, they ended up with marginal fields that could barely be used.

Many airports faced another problem: the traffic flows they had optimistically forecasted failed to materialize. Although both the airmail service and passenger numbers were on the rise, many airports were simply off the most active airways. There was justified grumbling that airports were more than a local, municipal concern and their cost was greater than what municipalities could bear alone. There were calls for a national air transport plan to straighten out what was increasingly seen as Herbert Hoover's laissez-faire mess, and demands for federal funding to help pay for it.

Compounding the airports' problem was the chill wind of the Great Depression. Airport financing came to a virtual standstill. Aviation stocks that had risen a thousandfold were worth pennies. Many struggling commercial aviation ventures failed, and many of the underfunded airports were in financial crisis. But as in all recessions, there were also well capitalized survivors who kept the infrastructure sputtering along. And the airports were about to get a boost from a most unlikely source: a Democratically-controlled federal government dedicated to creating jobs and sensing a great opportunity to do so by paving the nation with federally funded concrete runways.

Chapter Three
The Airport Matures

Albuquerque's adobe-revival terminal was one of the first attempts at giving airport architecture a local dimension and some flair beyond bland functionality. It still exists, although the airport it served has been long turned over to developers in favor of a new, larger airport.

In the fall of 1933 New York's mayor, Fiorello LaGuardia, was flying home from vacation in Florida. On the trip's final leg, originating from Pittsburgh, Pennsylvania, his TWA DC-2 landed uneventfully at Newark Airport, but after it taxied to the terminal the feisty little mayor refused to get off. When TWA's worried ground staff politely asked him if anything was wrong he said his ticket said New York, not New Jersey, and demanded to be flown to Floyd Bennett Field in Brooklyn, which was not served by the airlines.

There was an awkward standoff for just long enough to allow a pack of reporters and press photographers to pile onboard, and then the mayor got his

Chicago Municipal Airport's first terminal was built in the International Style. It is an expanded version of the Ford terminal in Dearborn, Michigan, which is regarded as the first example of a modern air terminal in the United States. The brand new DC-2 stands by as a Ford Trimotor boards its passengers. This terminal became inadequate as traffic increased but was not replaced until after World War II.

wish. It was all a clever publicity stunt, of course, which caught TWA off guard. It dramatically made the mayor's point that New York City didn't have its own airport suitable for airline service. Floyd Bennett Field, opened in 1931, was the city's official municipal airport, but the major airlines shunned it because it was too far from Manhattan to be accepted by the Post Office as an airmail terminus, and airmail was the airlines' main source of profit.

The mayor campaigned relentlessly for an alternative airport and set his sights on North Beach Airport in Queens on Long Island Sound, owned and operated by the Curtiss-Wright Corporation. It was a modest, general aviation airfield, but it served flying boats as well as landplanes and was only a 25-minute drive from Manhattan.

A multimillion-dollar construction project and land reclamation effort would be required to turn North Beach into an airport capable of handling the new, modern airliners which Douglas couldn't build fast enough to meet demand, but the mayor

wasn't deterred. And when in 1939 he presided over the opening of "his" state-of-the-art airport, which captured national attention and would soon be named after him, he could savor a particularly satisfying achievement. He had gotten the federal government to build and pay for most of it.

The creation of LaGuardia Airport symbolizes how radically the federal government's role changed in developing, financing, and supervising airports during the 1930s, when Franklin D. Roosevelt's Democratic administration discarded Herbert Hoover's associative state in favor of massive federal intervention in state affairs. This transformation was foremost an emergency reaction to the Great Depression, to quickly create jobs through public works. But regarding airports it also signaled the maturing of the nation's commercial air transportation system, which required more resources for airports than could be mustered by municipal financing and funding from the private sector.

According to the records compiled by the Department of Commerce's Aeronautics Branch, by

1931 there were approximately 1,200 airports in the United States, not counting the airways' emergency landing fields. Since 1926, when the drive for municipal ownership of airfields got underway in earnest, municipal fields had rapidly caught up in numbers with privately owned fields, accounting for approximately half of the total number of airports throughout the country. But it was gradually becoming evident that for various reasons an increasing number of both municipal and private fields were failing to live up to the promise rosily forecast for them by misguidedly optimistic founders. Simply put, practically no airport in the country was making enough money to pay for its keep, and the deepening depression was threatening to make things a lot worse.

"Build it and they will come," was the airport boosters' mantra in the second half of the 1920s. "It ain't necessarily so," they were painfully reminded by a popular tune by the 1930s. Airline traffic wasn't growing at nearly the rate forecast by the boosters. The lines carrying the airmail had a need for relatively few airports, mostly concentrated along the main arteries of commercial activity. And the demand for personal flying didn't come close to making a significant contribution to the airports' bottom line. Airfields established in out-of-the-way places languished barely used, and even the airports around the big population centers weren't profitable in spite of a fair amount of activity.

Many airports, particularly fields serving small towns with limited financial resources, also suffered because they were enthusiastically established on a shoestring without a realistic appreciation of the expenses required to properly build and operate them. Strained municipal budgets or finite private funds severely restricted the flow of additional financing when reality set in. This led to compromises, such as foregoing proper drainage systems, minimizing terminal and hangar facilities, and

In 1934 Pan American moved its center of operations from Miami Airport, which it owned, to Dinner Key in downtown Miami, because Pan Am had shifted exclusively to using flying boats to connect the Caribbean and South America with the United States. The terminal, designed by Delano and Aldrich, was the architects' second commission for Pan American and was hailed as an outstanding building. Four flying boats could board simultaneously. The building survives today as Miami's city hall.

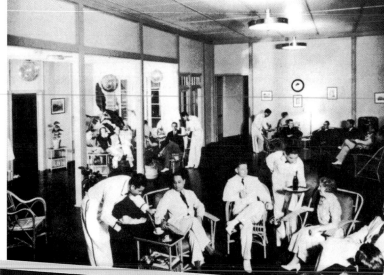

Above: The interior of Pan American's Dinner Key terminal captures the atmosphere of international air travel in the 1930s. It was the first to feature the large globe, which was as much a testimonial to Pan Am founder Juan Trippe's ambitions as it was a guide for passengers and spectators to the airline's global routes. All major Pan Am terminals had similar globes.

Above right: If the couple flying to Hawaii continued on to points west across the Pacific, they stayed in guest houses overnight en route, like this one on the island of Guam. Juan Trippe took great care to project his vision of Pan Am's image throughout its network and hired Delano and Aldrich to design the airline's guest houses at its Pacific island stops.

A Coca-Cola advertisement uses the exciting, progressive world of airline flying to push its product. Coke actually was beneficial to settle the stomachs of nervous passengers and refresh sleepy pilots and cabin crew for departure on a lazy afternoon. Less known is the fact that Asa Candler, the inventor of Coca-Cola, eventually sold to Atlanta, on favorable terms to the city, the field that became Hartsfield Airport.

limiting maintenance and fueling services, which rendered many an airport practically useless for sustained commercial operation.

Initially, airport owners and managers had fairly vague notions about generating income, which didn't go much beyond charging some usage fees or facility leases to regular users such as scheduled airlines. Now they strove to maximize their sources of revenue in response to the largely unexpected financial squeeze. They refined fee structures for regular customers and devised ways to charge additional fees to all users. Hangar rental fees, parking fees, landing fees, fuel and oil sales, airport taxes on these sales, and fee-based fueling and maintenance concessions all became standard practices and continue to be important revenue sources for all airports in some form or fashion to the present.

Other sources of revenue that seem less conventional today were also aggressively pursued. In the 1930s and for years to come, aviation remained a spectator event which created revenue possibilities. Airports large and small established airport restaurants aimed primarily not at air travelers but locals in search of a fine dining experience combined with the exciting possibility of watching the airplanes come and go. The Skyway Inn at Curtiss-Steinberg Field in Cahokia, Illinois (surviving as St. Louis Downtown Airport today), included with dinner night flying at a penny per pound of the passenger's weight, and pitched itself as a host for luncheon clubs and private banquets.

Privately owned Grand Central Airport in the Glendale suburb of Los Angeles, California, relied on show business for drawing spectators with spending money to the airport. The arrival and departure of Hollywood stars was announced on the public address system, inciting the star-struck to belly up to the ramp-viewing fence. For the more adventurous, three Fokker Trimotors were available for six-minute joy rides, with each passenger charged by weight, a penny a pound. The rides averaged 5,000 takers a month, grossing the airport a considerable sum for a sideline. On Sundays, Glendale, as the airport was popularly known, reached into aviation's not-too-distant past to attract the crowds. It put on an afternoon airshow

featuring parachutists, stunt fliers, and even crop-dusting demonstrations.

Other airports hoped to attract visitors to make a day of it at the airport by offering picnic grounds and for-profit recreational facilities. Birmingham Airport in Alabama had an 18-hole golf course adjacent to the field. Philadelphia's Camden Airport offered a swimming pool. Oakland airport in California built the country's first airport hotel. Several airports installed gas stations to service their visitors' automobiles, and a few started charging for parking. Kansas City's privately owned Fairfax Field seized upon a novel fee-income opportunity by setting up pay toilets that earned as much as $2,400 a year.

The Spanish Colonial Revival terminal at San Francisco Airport opened in 1938 to critical acclaim, finally giving the typical affluent passenger a terminal in line with expected aesthetic standards. The joke was on the passengers, though, because the terminal was built almost entirely in cheap cement, down to the exposed beams that were perfectly cast and tinted to look like wood.

The landside view of Pan American's Dinner Key terminal at Miami shows a full parking lot. Many of the car owners have just come to watch the excitement of the arrival of the afternoon Sikorsky S-40 flying boat originating from Buenos Aires, Argentina.

Fairfax was just about the only profitable airport in the nation, but only because of a fluke: Its owners struck natural gas on the airport premises.

But Fairfax's natural gas and pay-toilet bonanzas aside, the efforts to generate profits from operations failed at other airports because the volume of traffic wasn't sufficient. And then the Great Depression wiped out the net worth of many high-flying aviation companies.

Investment in airports dove in formation with the economy. In 1930 airports could still attract $30 million in investment for new construction and improvements, but that was largely money committed and set aside before the crash. In 1931 new investment halved to $14 million, and by 1932 it had imploded to $5 million.

As investment in airports virtually dried up, and municipalities began defaulting on airport bonds, salvation came from a most unlikely source: the federal government. Desperate to create jobs for the vast armies of the unemployed, President Franklin D. Roosevelt and his administration initiated a

massive public works program, and the airports succeeded in attracting their share of projects.

FDR didn't set out to save the airports or any other business for its owners' or operators' sake. His sole objective was to put as many people to work as possible at a wage that would provide them with some form of subsistence living. The airports were merely one of several means to this end. The most expedient way to create jobs was to launch public works projects that required large numbers of unskilled laborers. Anyone who needed a job could be handed a pick or a shovel and instantly put to work. One ideal opportunity for such make-work lay in improving airport runways and building new ones. So along with initiating a wide range of other public works projects, FDR's alphabet soup of relief organizations set out to pave the nation with runways.

The first organizations to provide airport relief were the Federal Emergency Relief Administration (FERA) and the Civil Works Administration (CWA) created under the auspices of the Federal

Newark's Art Deco terminal, which opened in 1936, gained much publicity because of the airport's prominent position serving New York City. It remains one of the most important buildings of the nation's airline heritage. Known as Building 1, it has recently been sympathetically restored.

Emergency Relief Act of 1933. Both organizations were temporary, conceived in a near panic to respond to the national economic emergency. FERA simply shoveled federal dollars to the states, which in turn doled out the funds for public works at their discretion. CWA also funded the states, but along with the funds it imposed a federal bureaucracy that had control over approving the projects to be supported by the government's contribution. Both organizations were temporary relief measures, replaced in 1935 by the more thoughtfully organized, larger, longer term Work Projects Administration (WPA).

To be eligible for FERA and CWA assistance, an airport had to be owned or leased by a munici-

Ironically, the Curtiss and Wright companies combined forces after their bitterly adversarial founders moved on. The joint company continued to expand aggressively, blanketing the nation with flying schools, hoping to raise a captive customer base.

Passengers of all kinds were showing up at airports by the 1930s. This United Airlines publicity shot reassures pet owners going by air that Fido need not stay behind or ride alone by train.

pality, or, if the project was to create a new airport, the municipality had to provide the land. Another condition was that 80 percent of a project's costs had to go for paying wages, insuring that most of these projects were to be low-tech earthworks or similar ventures. There was also a requirement for the municipalities receiving aid to match as much as half of the federal funds to provide the municipalities with an incentive to be responsibly engaged in the project.

Rather than arbitrarily consider airport projects proposed by the states, the CWA cooperated with the Bureau of Air Commerce to create a structured program for landing field improvements. This was in line with the continuing positive attitude toward the long-term prospects of commercial aviation among government officials despite the difficult economic times. The CWA found a particularly cooperative ally in Eugene Vidal, the newly appointed head of the Bureau of Air Commerce.

Bowlines away, next stop San Juan! A Commodore flying boat prepares for takeoff on nature's best runway from Dinner Key on its scheduled rounds of the Caribbean.

Vidal was an enthusiastic aviation booster, inspired by FDR's famous vision of a chicken in every pot to see a future with an airplane in every garage. Vidal was romantically obsessed with the prospects of the personal airplane and devoted a considerable amount of his office's time to sponsor a design competition to create one. This interest influenced his attitude toward the CWA's airport relief projects. By 1934 the CWA had 808 airports under construction or improvement, but in line with Vidal's vision of the personal airplane as mass transportation, many of these projects were at airports serving towns with populations of under 5,000 inhabitants.

These projects began to at least help tide over many an airport through the era's difficult economic times, but more importantly, they set a precedent that was in direct opposition to the rules laid down by the Air Commerce Act of 1926, which decreed that airports were strictly a municipal responsibility. Through FERA and the CWA, for the first time the federal government provided financing for municipal airports.

This precedent was strengthened further with the creation of the WPA in 1935, which assumed the responsibilities of the stopgap CWA. The WPA consolidated its control over the projects it oversaw. It created a Division of Airways and Airports and required participants to meet increasingly rigorous federal standards established by the Bureau of Air Commerce to be eligible for funding.

The WPA also required that municipalities own outright the airfields for which they sought aid, and continued the requirements for matching municipal funding and Bureau of Air Commerce approval of WPA projects. With these actions it informally laid the groundwork for the federal regulation of airports and the federal-municipal partnership of airport financing and operations that survive to the present.

The requirement for outright ownership of an airport to be eligible for federal funding created a severe problem for several airports, including Mines Field in San Francisco and Dayton Airport, both on land leased from private owners. The cities had to buy the land to get federal funding, but it wasn't an easy or quick task to complete the purchases.

PIARCO GUEST HOUSE

. . . exclusively for
PAN AMERICAN WORLD AIRWAYS
passengers

Port of Spain
TRINIDAD

FORM A-294—60M-48—PRINTED IN U.S.A.

Pan American built its own airports complete with guest houses and hotels overseas as it spread its route network across the globe. Night flying, especially night arrivals and departures, were less frequent on international routes than on the well-marked domestic airways, and passengers often stayed overnight at the day's last stop.

In the meantime, the civil aviation industry continued to make rapid technical progress. At long last the aviation boosters' cherished dreams were about to come within reach. Advances in aerodynamics, metallurgy, engine performance, and radio technology put the industry on the threshold of a new era that would usher in the modern, profitable airliner and would turn commercial aviation into one of the 20th century's most successful technological achievements.

The continuing development of commercial aviation during the depression remained feasible in spite of great aggregate economic misery because of two factors: First, the government continued to believe in its future and maintained a steady airmail budget. Second, traveling by air remained a mode of transportation for the upper echelons of business travelers and the moneyed elite which was sufficiently depression-proof to afford and eagerly embrace the unprecedented advances about to come in speed, comfort, reliability, and nationwide reach.

The airliner that changed the world was the Douglas DC-3. Its story is widely known, but its impact on the commercial aviation industry, including the development of airports, is worth recapping. Most importantly, it was the first airliner capable of making a profit without an airmail subsidy. Its two high-performance engines and svelte, aerodynamic aluminum airframe could lift a substantially higher load relative to its weight and could fly it faster and farther than its predecessors. With 21 seats on board, it was first to be able to carry enough passengers whose fares added up to more than it cost the airline to operate the flight.

Although the technology to make the DC-3 was readily available, the day's designers and airline executives didn't clearly identify its profit potential

A Varney Speed Lines amphibian air taxi pulls into Oakland on its hop across the bay from San Francisco. It will extend its landing gear and taxi right out of the water onto the ramp to drop off its passengers. Amphibians were used in waterside cities in the 1930s like helicopters are used today, because all they needed was a small pad to park.

up front. It was a classic case of fast-moving technology outpacing the ability of its users to grasp its potential. The designers at Boeing, which beat Douglas to the application of the newest technologies with the Boeing 247, deliberately reduced the size of its initial design to a 12-seater because of concern that the original aircraft would be too large for many of the nation's airports.

Donald Douglas himself first created the more modest 12-14 seat DC-2 for TWA. He was then approached by C. R. Smith, chairman of American Airlines, to make a larger version of the DC-2 that could be used as an overnight sleeper aircraft for 14 passengers. It was only after this version, the Douglas Sleeper Transport (DST), was in production that all involved realized that with 21 seats in a day configuration they had created the DC-3, the first airliner that could make money.

All the major airlines clamored for the DC-3 when it entered service in 1936 with American Airlines. Together with a relatively large number of Boeing 247s and DC-2s that preceded it by a few

TWA's transcontinental sleeper service prepares to leave Newark airport in this rare color photograph from the late 1930s by Ivan Dimitri. Passengers would be sipping freshly squeezed orange juice in Glendale, California, by the next morning if all went well.

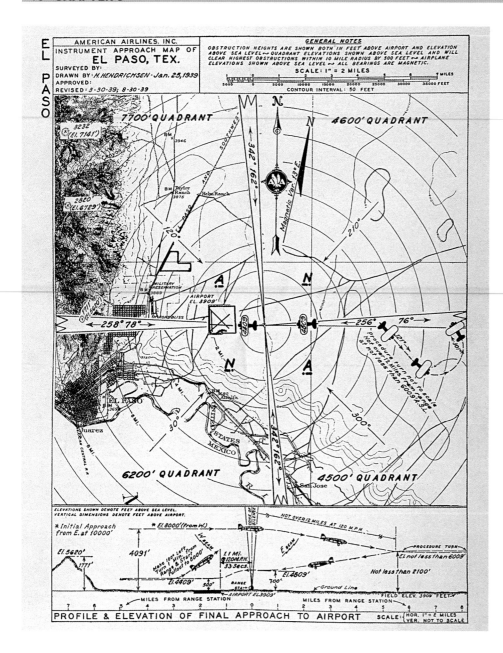

An American Airlines approach plate to El Paso, Texas, in 1939 shows how far blind flying by radio navigation had come in a little over a decade since the first experiments at College Park, Maryland. Despite routinely letting down on an approach to within 300 feet of the ground in the worst weather, airlines had become as safe as trains.

brought. In 1930 the U.S. airliners flew 32 million passenger miles. In 1937, a year after the DC-3 was introduced, they flew 459 million passenger miles. This was the point when airline transportation became a viable industry.

The higher performance aircraft, increasing numbers of passengers, and more frequent flights put greater demands on airports in several ways. Longer runways were required to handle the new airliners, and to be effective in all seasons and weather conditions the runways had to be paved. The increasing volume of traffic and safety considerations required advances in air traffic control, navigation, radio communication, weather information, and field services. And the growing number of passengers required the construction of bigger and more elaborate air terminals to accommodate them.

All these additional demands on the airports required a lot of money. Even in the best of times the municipalities wouldn't have had the resources to cope with these expanded responsibilities, and the Depression was still deepening toward its low point. The WPA continued to be willing to sink substantial government funds into the municipal airports, which was welcome, but airport and town managers felt it was time to officially discard the restrictions of the Air Commerce Act of 1926 and formalize the substantial federal role in the financing and oversight of airports that had been developing through the public works relief projects.

In 1937 at the meeting of the American Municipal Association and the National Conference of Mayors, those attending made a forceful pitch for change. They argued that airports were part of the national airway system. Airports benefited the national economy to a significantly greater degree than local interests. Their growing level of sophistication and needs created by increasing air traffic placed financial demands on the municipalities that could not be fully met. The federal government should therefore step in and formally assume its fair share of the financial responsibility for the nation's publicly owned airports.

Airport owners and operators were also becoming increasingly vocal about the changes they felt were necessary in the assistance they received

years, the DC-3 began to transform airline travel from a seemingly risky adventure into a revolutionary but reliable form of transportation.

The number of passengers skyrocketed with the introduction of the modern airliner and the higher capacity, greater speed, and greater reliability it

through the WPA projects. A consensus was emerging that airports needed more than could be achieved by the labor-intensive construction projects utilizing largely unskilled workers. There was a growing requirement for skilled, technical assistance and associated capital investment to implement on a national scale the developments in navigation, communication, and airport operations.

The technological advances since the 1920s and the spreading realization of what the future unlocked by the DC-3 was likely to bring raised industry-wide issues that went beyond the growing pains affecting the airports. There was also increasing concern about the Bureau of Air Commerce's ability to oversee the growth of civil aviation, spotlit by its indecisive handling of a series of major air crashes which resulted in the resignation of Eugene Vidal.

His replacement, Fred Fagg, was legal counsel and rising star of the Federal Aviation Commission, which was holding hearings on the future of air transportation. Fagg believed in the need for a planned, formal, national transport policy and had convinced the Commission that air commerce should be overseen by an independent federal agency. He succeeded in reinvigorating the Bureau of Air Commerce and threw himself into championing a

The airport postcard became immensely popular. The colorfully depicted terminal images even caught the fancy of spectators who would drive to an airport just to look around and send postcards depicting it to all their friends and relations.

The German airship *Hindenburg* is moored at Lakehurst Naval Air Station after one of its crossings from Germany in 1936. Lakehurst was the only civilian airship terminal in the United States, and the *Hindenburg* provided the only civilian airship service. In 1937 it exploded at Lakehurst after the season's first crossing, bringing the service to an abrupt end. The hangar still stands.

Fort Worth's new terminal is featured on the cover of this American Airlines employee magazine in 1937. Note the air conditioner truck pumping cold air into the DC-3 behind the fuel truck—pretty good service for 1937.

AMERICAN
HORIZONS

SEPTEMBER · 1937
PUBLISHED MONTHLY BY AMERICAN AIRLINES, INC.

formally recognized, federally supervised national air transportation system.

The consensus was slowly building for a major overhaul of the Air Commerce Act of 1926. Within the broader framework of civil aviation, supporters of federal financing for airports sensed the time had arrived to formalize the precedent-setting federal funding already taking place under the WPA relief projects.

The result of all this pressure for change was the Civil Aviation Act of 1938 that redefined the structure of civil aviation in the United States. It created the Civil Aviation Authority (CAA), a new, independent, federal entity explicitly dedicated to the oversight and regulation of civil aviation, including a national system of air transportation. A five-person group oversaw the Authority and regulated airline tariffs and route allocations, and an office of the Administrator managed the airway system and aviation safety. Within two years this structure was refined. The five-person group became the Civil Aviation Board, regulating airline fares and route allocations, and the Administrator's office became the Civil Aviation Administration in charge of all other civil aviation matters.

The CAA embarked on the task of enhancing, expanding, and further standardizing the operating regulations governing civil aviation. It set new safety and operations standards and rules, and revised the classification of airports into five new, simplified categories.

For municipal airport operators, the Civil Aviation Act of 1938 was exceedingly important for another reason. It established a federal role for the development, operation, and financing of airports in partnership with local authorities.

The Act came to the aid of municipal airports with an elaborate legal justification to appease states' rights advocates concerned about encroachment by the federal government on state affairs. It recognized municipal airports as an element of the national navigation system because they were places for taking off and landing for the purpose of picking up and discharging passengers and cargo within the system.

Above: The Eastern Airlines terminal at Boston Municipal Airport catered to DC-3s and remained standing long after the airport was renamed Logan.

A TWA terminal interior in the 1930s is brought alive by a rare color photograph. The simple check-in counter with the ubiquitous baggage scales is not all that different from the counters today, and the wall and column colors are also enjoying a retro-revivial.

Airship Ports

In the 1920's all signs indicated that the most promising long-range air vehicle would be the rigid airship. Its ability to stay aloft for days and carry a much larger load than any contemporary airplane made it ideal for flights of thousands of miles—flights that were otherwise impossible.

In 1928 the German airship *Graf Zeppelin* introduced long-range luxury passenger service with a spectacular nonstop demonstration flight across the Atlantic from Germany to the United States via the Azores. It carried 20 passengers and 41 crew. Opulently fitted out with a lounge/dining salon and private cabins, it had more in common with ocean liners than the airliners to come. When it completed its 111-hour, 6,800-mile flight—the longest by any aircraft at the time—it touched down at America's principal airship port, at Lakehurst, New Jersey.

Naval Air Station Lakehurst was established as an airship base in 1920, for in America airships were an obsession of the U.S. Navy. The U.S. Naval Airship Service was founded in 1917, and by the next year it was operating 16 non-rigid inflatable airships built by Goodyear in Akron, Ohio, on maritime patrol up and

The airship *Graf Zeppelin* sits in the massive hangar at Naval Air Station Lakehurst, New Jersey, after its maiden transatlantic crossing in 1928, and captures the invitation-only crowd's attention.

down the U.S. East Coast. With millions of square miles of ocean to patrol across the Pacific to Hawaii and the Philippines, the navy was also keen to employ the much larger, longer-range rigid airships like the *Graf Zeppelin*.

Airship bases were readily identifiable by their immense hangars, in which the craft were maintained and stored. The bases' other principal feature was the mooring mast to which the surprisingly maneuverable airship's nose was secured. The arrival procedure was to descend close to the ground, approach the mast, and toss dozens of lines to a waiting ground crew below. The ground crew would stabilize the behemoth and work together with the ship's crew to ease the airship to the mooring mast, where a waiting mooring crew would secure it.

Therefore, proclaimed the legal spin, the actual place of takeoff and landing was entitled to be established, developed, improved and financed by the federal government, as was any related technical equipment indispensable for the operation and safety of the airport, such as navigation aids, radio equipment, and lighting. Furthermore, the government had the right and responsibility to set and enforce all the rules of the operation of this section of the airport.

This interpretation, codified in the new legislation, was a rejection of the dock concept that held airports to be a municipal responsibility similar to ports. It did, however, leave the municipalities a significant role as well. It considered those parts of the airport which were not crucial to the direct, physical operation of aircraft to be a continuing municipal obligation.

Thus, the municipalities retained their responsibility for the air terminals, hangars, parking lots, and other related structures. It also remained their responsibility to provide the real estate for the airport. The states retained responsibility for the passage of appropriate state laws and regula-

On the ground the airship rested on a set of wheels perpendicular to its length. The mooring attachment holding its nose was freewheeling. As the wind changed, the airship would gently weathervane to face into it, minimizing the risk of wind damage.

Naval air stations appeared on both coasts as the service geared up for its new mission, and the Goodyear company established a joint venture with Zeppelin to build an advanced class of rigid airships. But the Navy wasn't lucky with its rigid airship program. An early model made in England was destroyed by mishandling during flight testing, and three of four others crashed in violent weather by 1935 without getting past the operational trial stage.

After its first visit to Lakehurst, the *Graf* went on a round-the-world trip and then entered scheduled service between Germany and South America, which it maintained for a decade before being retired from service.

Lakehurst lived through one golden year with the *Graf*'s much larger sibling, the *Hindenburg*, which completed ten flawless scheduled roundtrip Atlantic crossings in 1936. All fifty passenger berths were sold out both ways. Its lucky travelers were flown between Lakehurst and Newark in American Airlines' DC-3s to faster link-up with New York City or connect with domestic flights. The *Hindenburg*'s fiery explosion at Lakehurst on arrival after the 1937 season's first crossing ended the passenger airship era and Lakehurst's role as a civilian airship port.

The navy gave up on its rigid airships when the last one crashed in 1935, but continued to operate the inflatable ones with great success. At the height of World War II the navy had 168 of them in service, and its last airships flew until 1962. Small civilian inflatable airships continue to be popular advertising and camera platforms, but the airship ports of old are gone. Several of the hangars survive, including the one at Lakehurst and Hangar

Hangar One at Moffet Field in California still overshadows the base administrative building and is a national landmark.

One at Moffett Field near San Francisco. Both are designated national landmarks.

tions required for airport operations, and for development planning.

The federal government extended its powers over airports in another important respect. It secured far-reaching authority to approve airport development and improvement projects, including many of those aspects that remained state and municipal responsibilities. It justified this power grab on the grounds that because an airport was part of a national system, the authority with ultimate overall control had to have final approval if the system's needs were to be met efficiently.

One consequence of these developments was the gradual reduction in importance of the privately owned airport for the purpose of providing public air transportation. Without access to federal funding it was inevitable that the number of privately owned airports would decline to the point that they serviced only two niches: Small, private airports continued to serve private groups of sport pilots in areas where municipal airports were not conveniently available, and aircraft manufacturers continued to maintain private airports at plant locations for their own purposes.

Another TWA DC-3 touches down at Glendale. Passengers could spot friends and relatives waiting for them by the fence as the airplane taxied in.

In general, the division of federal-local responsibilities regarding airports that emerged from the Civil Aviation Act of 1938 continues to survive today. Both federal and local authorities provide funding for airports. Local or state authorities continue to own them. And the federal government supervises and regulates them as part of the national air transportation system.

Even as the flood of federal emergency relief funds orchestrated by FDR's administration enabled the country's municipal airport system to expand during the Great Depression, a handful of private airports serving concentrations of the wealthy also found the funds to grow. Together these municipal and private airports began to develop a sense of identity and distinctive styles of terminal architecture that would turn them into nationally recognized landmarks as the airlines became the most glamorous way to travel.

Two notable private initiatives at the forefront of the emerging trend in distinctive terminal architecture were at land-based airports in Los Angeles, California, in the early 1930s. They were the terminals at United Airport in Burbank, and Grand Central Airport in Glendale, both completed before they could have been put on hold by the full impact of the Depression.

Burbank Airport was built by United Airlines, then owned by Boeing, to serve as its prestigious main West Coast terminus. Its two-story Spanish Colonial revival-style terminal was one of the first modern passenger terminals and became nationally known through heavy publicity. In a greatly altered state it still stands today.

Glendale, which had been a colorful gathering place since 1921 for every kind of flyer in the Los Angeles basin, from aircraft designers and racing pilots operating on shoe-string budgets to well-heeled private fliers from high society, became the Los Angeles terminal for TWA and American Airways. Its airline terminal, completed in 1930, was best known for its gem of an Art Deco tower featuring winged women atop each of its four corners. The terminal was in the Spanish Colonial revival style so popular in California.

Curtiss Flying Service erected a less progressive but equally distinctive structure south of Los Angeles at Mines Field, as that company relentlessly pursued its objective of having a presence at important airports nationwide. This structure, Hangar 1, was of steel construction ornamented with the ever popular Spanish Colonial façade and towers. Its terminal was attached in an old fashioned lean-to arrangement. Hangar 1 is a cargo office at LAX today.

One of the first airport projects of the 1930s on the East Coast to capture national attention was another private initiative, Pan American's Miami, Florida, seaplane base at Dinner Key. Backed by his deep-pocketed investors and generous international airmail subsidies, Juan Trippe relentlessly pursued his dream of a global airline and was determined not to let the Depression stifle his plans. As he reached beyond the short hop to Cuba and the neighboring Caribbean islands toward South America, his most suitable choice for long-range intercontinental aircraft was the flying boat.

Pan Am acquired its seaplane base at Dinner Key in 1930, when it took over the New York, Rio, and Buenos Aires line. NYRBA was operating twin-engined Consolidated Commodore flying boats on a regular schedule to its namesake Latin American cities but it lost out to Juan Trippe's greater business acumen. As Trippe secured his grip on his new acquisition and rapidly built on its routes, he needed substantial hangar facilities and a suitably impressive passenger terminal. He turned to Delano and Aldrich Architects of New York, who had constructed one of America's first distinctive air terminals, Pan Am's land terminal at Miami Airport.

Delano and Aldrich's Dinner Key terminal, completed in 1934, was an Art Deco showcase, a streamlined white gateway to the Caribbean and South America. Beckoning at the end of a sweeping, palm-studded driveway, it was the central anchor of the seaplane-base complex. It was flanked by boarding jetties on each side and cavernous, modern maintenance hangars beyond them. Its exterior projected bold, simple lines with gently curved edges, evocative of flying's direct, minimalist, form-follows-function design principles.

The terminal's interior featured a large, airy, one-level central hall with check-in and ticketing counters along the sides. Its main attraction was an enormous globe erected in the center of the floor on which passengers and visitors could follow Pan American's expanding international route network. The globe became a Pan American trademark, installed in many of its terminals worldwide in the 1930s.

Passengers walked out onto to the boarding docks, which could each accommodate two large flying boats at a time. Spectators seeing them off could watch the action from two rooftop observation decks.

Pan American ceased its flying boat operations at the end of World War II, but the terminal, an important architectural relic of the Art Deco period, is a Miami municipal office today.

On the West Coast another California airport, San Francisco's Mills Field, was slowly turning from little more than a cow pasture into a major metropolitan airport with the help of the WPA. Renamed San Francisco Airport in 1931, its potential lay in the possibility of reclaiming over 1,000 acres of shallow tidal flats from San Francisco Bay.

The development of the airport was a project tailor-made for the WPA. For the fiscal year of 1935-36, San Francisco Airport succeeded in securing $1.6 million in WPA funds to commence

a major land reclamation project to extend its runways. Along with resurfacing and widening the existing runways it would provide employment for over 5,000 laborers.

Concurrently with the allocation of WPA funds, the municipality of San Francisco contributed a much more modest $141,000 for the construction of a new terminal. Finished in 1937, it was a fine example of a municipality on a tight budget employing low-cost construction techniques for maximum effect.

The terminal was a large, handsome, two-story Spanish Colonial revival building with a palatial passenger hall opening onto a breezy arcade supported by pillared archways. Its passenger hall featured opulent interior detailing, particularly of the ceiling and floor. Although its exterior appearance suggested a plaster finish over traditional brick construction, the most meticulous expert observer was hard-pressed to tell that the terminal was built almost entirely of inexpensive, moldable concrete. Even the weathered redwood beams of the arcade's ceiling were painted, molded concrete. Its concrete floor was finished in an acid-stained bronzed green and brown pattern that passed for colored quarry tile.

The passenger hall's interior featured finishing treatments other than concrete, but also followed

A summer training camp for U.S. Army Air Corps reserve pilots is set up at Biloxi Airfield in Mississippi. The unpaved airstrip is behind the ballpark. Judging by the cars parked next to the tents, most of the pilots had wheels by 1939.

Toledo was proud of resurfacing its runways with heavy-duty concrete in anticipation of the heavier aircraft on the way, but its runway lengths would soon be inadequate to accommodate the new models, and the runways would have to be lengthened.

the tenet of achieving maximum effect at minimal expense. The walls were coated with plaster and had inlaid stone travertine accents. The opulent ceiling was molded plaster, painted and glazed to resemble more expensive finishing materials. The ticketing and check-in counters were black marble travertine, the stairs green travertine, and railings and other accents Spanish antique-style wrought iron.

The end result was an indispensable step beyond the early airport woodshed look. It created an ambience and standards expected by the wealthy travelers who had to be wooed if airline flying was to be profitable.

Newark Airport, which had become New York City's main airport handling all the airmail and four major airlines, benefited greatly from the WPA program beyond the expansion of runways and other airside facilities. It received $700,000 to build an administration building to process the large volume of airmail and handle other functions. Completed in 1935, it was one of the finest examples of Art Deco airport architecture. Broad expanses of glass alternated with the low-profile white wall of the building. A balcony sunk into the building's profile runs the length of the second floor on each side of the central section, which features oval awning accents and is capped by an oval glass control tower.

Inside, molded plaster is used in tastefully restrained fashion for ornamentation using classic curvilinear geometric shapes to evoke the image of wings and a sense of flight. The building has become a valued Art Deco relic and has recently been restored.

Chicago's Municipal Airport also got its first substantial terminal, a building in the simple, clean International Style, free of Art Deco curvature and ornamentation. It was designed by Chicago's city architect, Paul Gerhardt, Jr., and was a bigger, more elaborate version of the Ford terminal in Dearborn created by Albert Kahn.

WPA-assisted airport construction proliferated everywhere, keeping abreast of the growing air traffic on the main airways and laying the foundations for the future along the less busy routes. With the WPA's help, Kansas City and Lambert Field in St. Louis, Atlanta Municipal Airport, Jacksonville and Tampa in Florida, Oklahoma City in Oklahoma, Wichita's Mid Continent Airport in Kansas, and many other airports cemented their claim to a role in the bedrock of the nation's emerging airway system and civil aviation infrastructure.

The nation's system of airports was becoming mature enough to encourage the introduction of design features stressing a local flavor. The most obvious cases were California's airport buildings in the Spanish Colonial style, but the most striking example was Albuquerque's adobe air terminal.

Albuquerque, New Mexico, was a critically important stop on the southern transcontinental route from the beginning, when TAT and Western Air Express both built their own airports there to serve their flights crossing the forbidding Rocky Mountains. Following the merger of the two airlines, the city attempted to get approval for a municipal airport but had difficulties convincing the electorate until the Depression brought the WPA to the rescue in 1936.

Above: TWA's four-engined Stratoliner, the world's first pressurized airliner, draws the Boston crowds as it taxies out for departure undeterred by the soggy day. Within a few years this airplane would be pressed into military transport service and would routinely fly between New Delhi, India, and the U.S. East Coast via South America, West Africa, and the Middle East.

Left: By the end of the 1930s, private flying was serious business, and the big radial-engined cabin airplane, like this gull-winged Stinson Reliant, was the private jet of its age. It also attracted the Hollywood set, shown here before Glendale's magnificent Art Deco tower.

It was constructed in Pueblo Revival style with adobe block encasing the underlying reinforced concrete structure. Its brown baked earth walls and protruding wooden roof beams were a striking reminder to arriving passengers that they were entering an environment substantially different from the one they had left behind. The regional flavor was further enhanced by the terminal's Spanish Colonial interior décor popular in the Southwest.

While Albuquerque proudly watched as TWA's and American Airlines' most modern airliners pulled up to its adobe terminal, Washington, D.C., the nation's capital, was still without an official public airport. It was an absurd situation, but there was a good reason: the District of Columbia was federal land, and the Air Commerce Act of 1926 forbade the federal funding of airports.

Since the government was unwilling to grind through the contentious task of legislating an exception to this contradiction, the private sector stepped in, but not with the results hoped for in such situations by free market advocates. Two airports, Hoover Field and Washington Airport, were opened in succession across the street from each other in the 1920s on the Potomac River, on the site where the Pentagon stands today. But they had a spotty performance record and changed hands several times among under-funded private owners.

They were merged at last into Washington-Hoover Airport in 1930, but even combined, the field was too small and ill-equipped to be worthy of being the capital's airport. The road continued to bisect the combined airport and its main runway, requiring traffic lights to stop road traffic when an airplane was taking off or landing.

Arguments raged back and forth between various political factions about how to handle the problem. The precedent for federally funding airport construction induced by the Depression finally created the opportunity to build Washington, D.C., a suitable, government-owned airport. Structured as a joint WPA and Army Corps of Engineers project, its construction finally got underway in 1938. When it opened in June 16, 1941, Washington National Airport was one of the nation's most modern airports,

Washington, D.C., didn't get an airport worthy of the capital until 1941 because of legislative problems with financing it. Until 1938 the law allowed only municipalities to finance airports, and the capital was a federal area. When Washington National was finally built, it was a fitting addition to the capital's important facilities. Its key aesthetic element was a curtain of glass toward the airside that presented the Washington skyline to passengers.

Washington-Hoover Airport was Washington, D.C.'s first airport. It was privately built on a shoestring and wasn't considered worthy of serving the capital.

Albuquerque Municipal Airport became New Mexico's biggest work relief project. When it was completed in 1939, it presented to the traveling public one of the more aggressive early attempts to inject a local flavor into terminal design. The terminal was in conformity with the CAA's recommended layout and size for an airport like Albuquerque Municipal, but its aesthetic appearance was radically different from any other airport in the country.

conforming to the new standards then emerging for airport planning, design, and construction.

The site selected for Washington National, with strong influence from President Roosevelt, who was deeply involved in the whole project, was the marshy flat land known as Gravelly Point, just beyond Washington-Hoover Airport along the Potomac. Chosen for its close proximity to the center of Washington, which was only 4.5 miles away, it required major landfill work to reclaim from the surrounding marshes the 680 acres of mud flats that would constitute most of its 750-acre site. Land reclamation directed by the Army Corps of Engineers took up the first year of construction. A dike was erected around the proposed airport perimeter, and 20 million cubic yards of sand and gravel were pumped in to raise the field surface to 20 feet above sea level.

By the time Washington National was built, airports serving major metropolitan areas were becoming large, complex facilities with an expectation of high passenger volumes that would grow considerably in coming years. These prospects created the need and opportunity for airport terminal design to progress beyond cosmetically tinkering with a relatively standard layout, and enabled terminal design to break away from the influence of the railway station. Washington National's main building was among the first of this new breed of air terminal that met certain layout standards required by its function, but was a powerful architectural focal point unique to the airport it served.

Washington National's architects also faced a design challenge that reached beyond the terminal as a stand-alone project. Washington, D.C., was the only American city planned in a style more common in Europe, with carefully located prominent public buildings interconnected by sweeping avenues and public parks in a grand urban design. The airport was close enough to the city to have to fit into this scheme.

The lead architect, Howard L. Cheney, supervised by innumerable advisory boards, review commissions, and other assorted meddlers, succeeded admirably in integrating the terminal into the capital's ambience. He created a sweeping, curvilinear, Art Deco building made of reinforced

The dispatch room at Washington National kept track of flight information the old fashioned way, on a matrix on a giant blackboard. Simple it may have been, but in concept it wasn't all that different from the databases of today.

The landside façade of Washington National Airport's curvilinear terminal reflected the inspiration of the capital's federal buildings in texture, form, and color, but also integrated the federalist style of George Washington's Mount Vernon residence.

Mayor Fiorello LaGuardia's campaign begins to unseat Newark, New Jersey, as New York's primary airport. The white circle makes it clear why North Beach Airport, owned by Curtiss, will be the best thing for Manhattan when it is transformed into Mayor LaGuardia's proposed multimillion dollar airport.

concrete with two different facades serving different objectives, nestled into the gently rising terrain.

On the landside, its functional facade resembled many of the capital's public buildings in color, texture, and general outline. But its dominant colonnaded entrance, rising above wings to either side, also invoked the nation's history by subtly hinting at an earlier style found in nearby Mount Vernon.

On the airside, the terminal's facade was a three-story-high curtain of glass facing a sweeping view of the Washington skyline. Here the focus was on presenting the terminal's visitors a framed image of the outside. Passengers and spectators could admire the Washington monument, the Capitol's dome, and other prominent landmarks stretching beyond the silvery streamlined airplanes on the ramp below.

A prominent feature of the new terminal was its dining room on the floor above the main passenger

hall. With its inlaid blue terrazzo floor, its molded plaster ceiling, its wood-paneled interior wall, and open-air dining terrace with the stunning view, it was one of Washington's smartest restaurants for years to come. In its first year of operation it captured a fair share of the airport's more than two million visitors, of whom only 344,000 were passengers.

The terminal also had a President's Suite befitting the chief executive who laid the building's first cornerstone and was present at the airport's grand opening to watch a cunning American Airlines pilot touch down early to beat the scheduled Eastern flight to the first landing.

Washington National was also one of the most advanced airports in the country technologically. Its squat control tower contained the latest equipment in weather monitoring and air traffic control, and the airlines had a choice of four runways covering the prevailing wind directions. The 6,855-foot main

CITY OF NEW YORK
MUNICIPAL AIRPORTS
NO.1 FLOYD BENNETT FIELD · NO.2 NORTH BEACH
EAST RIVER SEAPLANE BASES   WALL STREET — 31ST STREET
F.H. LaGUARDIA
MAYOR
JOHN McKENZIE
COMMISSIONER OF DOCKS

As the development of North Beach Airport got underway, Mayor LaGuardia had this poster issued to tout New York's municipal airports and plant the idea in the population's mind that New York was the most important center of both seaplane and landplane service.

Above: Pan American's Marine Air Terminal served the airline's giant Boeing B-314 flying boats plying the Atlantic, represented by the flying fish motif. Another valuable Art Deco relic by Delano and Aldrich, the terminal continues to serve the airlines.
Right: Pan American's giant B-314 flying boat is preparing to leave LaGuardia's Marine Air Terminal for the Azores and points beyond in Europe.

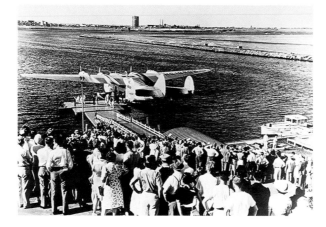

but within months of its opening it was renamed for the city's combative, tenacious mayor who was more responsible for creating it than anyone else.

New York City's first municipal airport was Floyd Bennett Field, opened in 1931 with high hopes of providing an alternative to Newark Airport in New Jersey, which was only half an hour from downtown Manhattan. Floyd Bennett Field was not a commercial success. Located in an isolated southern section of Brooklyn, it proved to be too far from Manhattan to lure anyone away from Newark. Plans for a fast, efficient transit system from Floyd Bennett Field to Manhattan never materialized, and the Post Office refused to make it New York's airmail terminus, issuing a final rejection 1936 to end a running battle with Mayor LaGuardia.

The mayor accepted losing the battle but not the war. He refocused his sights on North Beach Airport in Queens, owned by the Curtiss-Wright Company. It was a 105-acre site on Bowery Bay and had been passed over as too small by the previous administration when it was searching for the location that would become Floyd Bennett Field. But the location of North Beach Airport was perfect. As close, if not closer, in commuting time to downtown Manhattan as Newark, it was located on the major highway grid of New York's boroughs. In addition, its location on the waters of Long Island Sound made it perfect for accommodating the long-range intercontinental flying boats.

The only challenge, and one reason why the site was passed over earlier, was the need for a major landfill project to build the space required for it on the shallow reefs extending into Bowery Bay. But even this was seen as having some advantages. The reclamation could be done for a predictable cost, the area available was easily more than the airport would need, and most of the work could be handled as a much needed WPA project to put New York's unemployed to work.

In fact, once he had a clear vision of what North Beach Airport could become, LaGuardia turned the construction of his airport into the biggest single project undertaken by the WPA. Preliminary work commenced in late 1937, but construction got underway in earnest after President Roosevelt

runway was the longest— enormous by the standards of the day. The other runways were 5,210 feet, 4,892 feet, and 4,100 feet long, also well above the norm for the highest category of airport. One future drawback, which was scarcely an issue then, was the lack of room for runway expansion. It hasn't stopped the latest jets from accessing the airport, but has limited the number of daily flights the airport can handle.

While Washington National Airport incorporated the latest developments in airport design and construction and had a landmark terminal, the airport that set the standards above all others and flamboyantly showed the way into the 1940s and 1950s was New York City's LaGuardia Airport. It was first known by the blander sounding New York Municipal Airport, approved the full WPA commitment on September 3, 1938. Within days, Mayor LaGuardia himself was astride a steam shovel, ostensibly shoveling the first bucket of landfill for the reporter's cameras.

Most of the landfill came from the giant municipal garbage dump on nearby Rikers Island, from which a bridge was built to the site. The project was run at breakneck speed 24 hours a day in the hope of having the airport ready in time for the New York World's Fair in the summer of 1939 (it wasn't). Forty steam shovels loaded as many as 400 trucks on a schedule calculated to deliver a truckload of eight cubic yards of fill every seven seconds, 24 hours a day. By the time they were done, they had delivered over 17 million cubic yards of fill to reclaim 357 acres of the new airport's 558-acre site.

While the reclamation was under way, teams of WPA, city, and private civil engineers and architects finished the detailed plans for the airport. It was designed to be two airports in one: a landplane base and a seaplane base, each with its own terminal.

The New York City-based architectural firm of Delano and Aldrich got the contracts for both terminals. By this time Delano and Aldrich had accumulated considerable experience in terminal design, primarily through their work for Pan American. This project was the firm's opportunity to cement its reputation as the nation's leading airport architect.

Delano and Aldrich's landplane terminal was the prototype of the modern air terminal, employing a passenger-flow innovation that continues to be a standard feature of airports today. For the first time, arriving and departing passengers were separated vertically. Departures were dropped off on one level, arrivals picked up on the other. The advantage of dedicated arrival and departure floors is the unhindered, one-way flow of passengers, allowing for the smooth, rapid movement of high volumes of people, and offering an easy opportunity for future expansion.

This innovation had appeared a decade earlier in one of the plans submitted for the Leigh Portland Cement Airport Design Competition, but low passenger volumes hadn't warranted putting it into practice until the construction of LaGuardia.

The imposing rectangular entrance lead into a spacious rotunda. At its far side was the central

passenger hall. Wings to either side of the entrance housed administrative offices. A long, low structure stretching across the front of the terminal on the airside contained the boarding gates to the airliners lined up on the apron. The terminal had an upper-story central viewing area, and a rooftop viewing platform ran the length of the gate structure.

An upper floor in the central rotunda provided several restaurants and a bar, all managed by the New Yorker Hotel. They did a brisk business with a

LaGuardia's tower was considered to be the last word in control towers when the airport opened in 1940. The analogy to Grand Central Station shows how rail travel was still the benchmark against which other forms of travel were measured.

WINGS OF THE NIGHT OVER LAND & SEA AT LA GUARDIA AIRPORT

Aviation Terrace Restaurant
OPERATED BY HOTEL NEW YORKER, NEW YORK

First visit to La Guardia Airport Sunday, September 21, 1941 with Mr & Mrs Ewer

Dining at the best airport restaurants was as much of an occasion in the 1930s as going to the best restaurants in town. At LaGuardia, Manhattan's prestigious New Yorker Hotel had the concession to run all the dining and in-flight catering services. Diners came from all over the greater New York area to savor Lobster Thermidor on the dining terrace and watch the great silvery airlines come and go.

large customer base that still regarded the busy airport traffic as unique entertainment and considered dining at an elegant airport restaurant to be on par with frequenting the best restaurants in town.

In the aesthetic design of the Marine Air Terminal at LaGuardia, on the other side of the field from the landplane terminal, Delano and Aldrich got somewhat carried away. They modeled it on the Roman Pantheon to the delight of the architectural critics. The simple, round, domed building with light from

the heavens pouring in through the central skylight could evoke a pious atmosphere when conditions were right. It effectively transposed reverence for the ancient gods with the practically religious awe in which the public of the 1930s held the modern flying boat, setting out with compass, clock, and sextant for distant lands thousands of watery miles away.

The circular passenger flow worked well for the relatively low volume of daily flying boat passengers. It continues to be effective today as a central passenger distribution point to the spokes leading to the modern jetways. But the hassles of our modern, crowded skies have long banished any sense of piety the building may have once evoked.

Both terminal buildings were generously adorned with modern Art Deco motifs. The stylized eagle

LaGuardia's main terminal, designed by Delano and Aldrich, was the first airport terminal to separate arriving and departing passengers on different levels to make the flow of passengers more efficient.

featured prominently on the landplane terminal. Glazed reliefs of flying fish encircled the Marine Air Terminal. WPA funds extended to paying for interior art work for both facilities. Under a WPA program to support struggling artists, commissioned murals decorated both passenger halls. A rendition of the zodiac encircled the landplane terminal, while the history of flight was portrayed in the rotunda of the Marine Air Terminal.

While the terminals received the greatest share of popular attention, the most imposing technical achievement of LaGuardia Airport was the immense pentagonal maintenance hangar serving the flying boats adjacent to the Marine Air Terminal. An innovative structural design allowed trusses to radiate from one central pillar near the widest side of the structure, leaving the entire floor area completely free of supporting pillars, giving an uninterrupted covered area two football fields in size.

There were also two sets of three landplane hangars with lean-to multilevel office blocks running their length. These blocks met the administrative and other needs of the various airlines using the field.

LaGuardia was equipped with the latest technological innovations of the time. Its radio communications equipment was the most up to date, and it had one of the first instrument-landing systems in the world. Traffic was directed from a birdcage tower of the type that was becoming increasingly popular at the larger airports nationwide.

The two main runways were 6,000 feet and 5,000 feet respectively, laid out in a "T" shape. They are still in use today, extended to accommodate jets.

Opening day at LaGuardia on October 15, 1939, attracted 350,000 visitors. VIPs and military aircraft flew in from all over the country for the occasion. The airport had cost $40 million and was considered the country's most modern airport.

Two shorter runways provided additional alternatives for changing wind conditions.

LaGuardia officially opened on October 15, 1939. Its opening day celebrations were attended by 350,000 people. The final price tag was $40 million, of which the WPA's contribution was approximately $28 million, or 70 percent. At the height of its construction 23,000 WPA laborers worked on it round the clock in three shifts. They completed it in a little over two years after President Roosevelt had authorized the WPA's lead participation in creating it.

LaGuardia was truly America's first modern airport. And it was a fitting example of a top-class airport for the planned system of airports which, according to the CAA's 1939 airport study, the nation needed, and for which the CAA found federal expenditures appropriate.

Three of four airlines serving Newark—American, TWA, and United—immediately abandoned that airport for LaGuardia. The effect on Newark was devastating. It closed down shortly thereafter, forcing the lone holdout, Eastern Airlines, to follow its peers to LaGuardia Airport. Mayor LaGuardia had won his war of the airports.

But all was not lost for Newark or languishing Floyd Bennett Field. Both were saved by that great unfortunate catalyst of aviation; war. First, In 1941 Newark reopened temporarily when the big four airlines agreed to reestablish limited service there. But it regained its long-term lease on life in 1942 when the U.S. Army took it over for the duration of World War II. Newark's ultimate revenge is that today it is once again the New York City metropolitan area's busiest airport.

Floyd Bennett Field, conveniently on the shore of Jamaica Bay, drew increasing attention from the U.S. Navy, which took it over in 1941, commissioned it as Naval Air Station Floyd Bennett Field, and bought it outright from New York City a year later.

In the 1930s, through the WPA and other relief projects and finally through legislation, the U.S. government exerted federal control over America's airports. It established federal funding for them alongside continued municipal funding, creating new airports in the process and saving many from oblivion. The newly created federal bureaucracy, the Civil Aviation Administration, concluded that the nation needed a comprehensively planned and federally funded system of airports.

As America entered the 1940s it was about to get a system of airports more immense than anyone had ever envisioned, but with an important difference. It would be driven not by the needs of civil aviation but national defense.

When it was completed, LaGuardia had undergone an amazing transformation from the modest Curtiss flying field. It employed 28,000 WPA workers at the height of construction and swallowed 17 million cubic yards of landfill.

Chapter Four
Mass Air Transit

Washington National Airport got too crowded in the 1950s to keep its sweeping foyer free. Check-in counters took over the space, but passengers and visitors could still stroll out onto the balcony to watch the airplanes come and go.

I n 1956, in a special issue called "Air Age," *LIFE* magazine followed a day in the life of American commercial aviation. Between 3:00 P.M. on June 3 to 3:00 P.M. on June 4, the scheduled airlines operated 1,095 of their airliners on multiple flights and carried 136,823 passengers. The nation's six busiest airports, New York, Chicago, Washington, Los Angeles, Atlanta, and Dallas handled 1,707 arrivals, 1,669 departures, and 97,531 passengers. The article noted that only 30 years before, in 1926, the airlines had carried 5,782 passengers during the entire year.

LIFE found that commercial flying had become a way of life. It noted that the parents of a nine-year-old boy carrying a box of live lobsters entrusted him to the cabin crew of an American Airlines evening flight departing Boston for the West Coast. He was safely with his grandparents in Oregon by the following afternoon.

At Washington National Airport the Republican National Committee Chairman, returning from his third trip of the week to New York, told the magazine that he flew 300,000 miles a year. Senator John F. Kennedy was also spotted flying in. In Atlanta the caterer Dobbs House prepared 1,500 airline meals that day. A poodle, a puma cub, penguins, a boa constrictor, and a flamingo were among the live air cargo that crisscrossed the nation between various destinations. More conventional air cargo amounted to 3,800 tons for the day.

In Los Angeles passengers in a hurry landed at the airport and jumped into a waiting helicopter to hop downtown. At American Airlines' main maintenance base in Tulsa, Oklahoma, mechanics worked around the clock in three shifts to keep the company's propliners flying. And in Gettysburg, Pennsylvania, President Eisenhower opted for a 22-minute flight to Washington, D.C., in his personal twin-engined Aero Commander instead of a two-hour drive in the presidential limousine.

In large measure, *LIFE*'s passengers had come to take for granted the benefits of the tremendous technological advances American aviation had realized during World War II and the massive airport infrastructure the government had developed to support the war effort. A majority of today's large commercial airports were comprehensively upgraded or built from scratch during the war. Not before or since has there been a time of such large-scale airport construction in the United States.

America's recognition that it needed a planned national air transport system coincided with Europe's alarming slide toward another world war. When the Civil Aviation Authority was founded in 1938, a condition for establishing it was that it undertake a study to determine the need for a national system of airports and develop a National Airport Plan. The study, completed in 1939, found that the United States had only 76 Class III

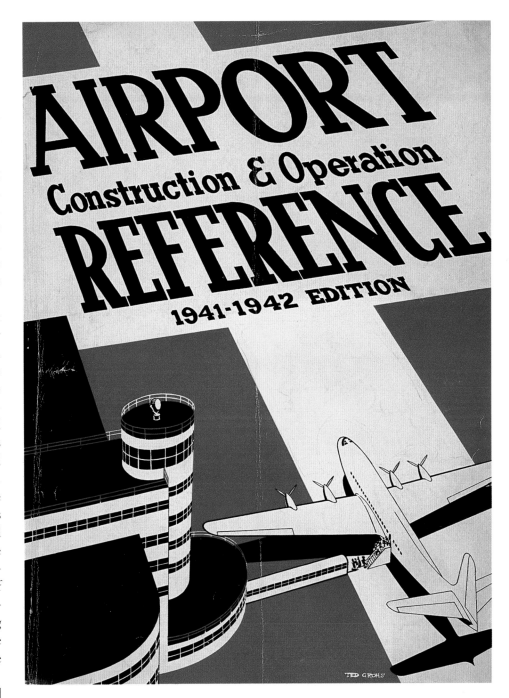

airports suitable for commercial airline operations and a handful that were ranked higher.

The ensuing National Airport Plan submitted to Congress anticipated significant air traffic growth and recommended the construction of 422 Class III and 48 Class IV airports. In the longer term it saw a need for the construction or improvement of up to 3,500 airports and audaciously projected a cost

This annual manual represents the importance of airport design and construction and reflects the anticipated arrival of the four-engined airliners, which required thoughtful forward planning.

Right: A pilot and copilot of a brand new B-26 bomber review their cross-country flight plan before takeoff at one of hundreds of airbases built in the country during World War II to handle the tens of thousands of aircraft made and pilots that needed to be trained.

Below: Home defense was a major concern after the Japanese surprise attack on Pearl Harbor, leading to extreme precautions. Burbank airport is expertly camouflaged. The apron is painted to look like a three-dimensional neighborhood from altitude. The neighborhood behind and to the left of the terminal is false, erected atop Lockheed's main plant. From time to time sentries rearranged fake cars on the streets to fool prying eyes.

approaching $500 million. As a stingy Congress mulled over this request, the plan was overtaken by events in Europe.

While America did little to prepare for World War II before the Japanese attack on Pearl Harbor on December 7, 1941, it did more than it is generally given credit for, with a particular focus on airports needed for national security. By 1939 the War Department was becoming increasingly alarmed by the deteriorating political situation overseas, and in August, weeks before the outbreak of World War II in Europe, it asked the U.S. Army Air Corps to compile a list of civilian airports suitable for national defense.

The Army Air Corps, infused with a heightened sense of urgency by the commencement of war in Europe, took the request seriously. Driven by a fear of potential German submarine activity off U.S. shores dating back to the experience of World War I, it made a sweeping recommendation to improve every East Coast airport within 150 miles of the ocean for military use. It also concluded that all Class III and higher civilian airports should be made usable by the military.

Following discussions between the Army Air Corps, the navy, the CAA, and the WPA, which continued to fund relief projects at both military and civilian airports, an interdisciplinary committee compiled a more detailed wish list of airports slated for improvement. It ended up listing about 4,000 of them and projected a cost of $550 million to perform the necessary work.

These efforts superseded the National Airport Plan for the duration of World War II. America would get its airports, more than anyone ever foresaw in peacetime. But the airport infrastructure that ultimately emerged was skewed geographically to military rather than civilian needs.

There were myriad requirements for converting an airport for military use or building one from scratch, depending on its intended mission. Needs may have included hangars, maintenance facilities, fuel farms, specialized capabilities such as ordnance handling and storage, communications and navigation aids, and housing and provisioning for the officers and enlisted personnel.

However, for every airport on the list the largest chunk of the projected costs was the requirement to construct heavy-duty runways that were 5,000 feet or longer. This was called for by the rapid increases in aircraft size, weight, and performance, and was the minimum runway length considered capable of handling the coming four-engined heavy bombers and transports. The Air Corps was about to place its first big order for the Boeing B-17 bomber, which had been flying since 1936; and the Douglas DC-4 and Lockheed Constellation four-engine transports were already on the drawing board.

With the depression still gripping the country and widespread opposition in the United States to participating in Europe's war, Congress wasn't overly keen to write a $550 million check to militarize airports. Anticipating political realities, the Committee submitted a more modest initial request of $80 million through the CAA in the fall of 1940, and Congress grudgingly approved half that amount for bringing 250 civilian airports up to military standards.

The airlines played a major domestic transport role during the war, and the airports they used got significant airside facility upgrades, primarily longer, stronger, and more runways.

Van Nuys Airport was lined with military transports at the end of World War II. The four-engined C-54s are awaiting conversion into civilian DC-4s. The C-47s will become DC-3s. The conversion companies couldn't work fast enough to meet pent-up demand for airliners.

The improvements were to be carried out jointly by the CAA, the WPA, the Army Air Corps, and the navy under the auspices of a new program called the Development of Landing Areas for National Defense, or DLAND for short. DLAND became a major contributor to the war effort at home, ultimately expending approximately $400 million for airport improvements nationwide.

By 1943 the need for soldiers and workers for the war effort had seen to it that unemployment relief was no longer needed for the first time since 1929. The long-serving WPA ended and DLAND continued on without it.

In addition to the DLAND program and the joint use of airports with civilian operations, the military also took over existing airports entirely, for the duration of the war, typically under some lease arrangement. These takeovers occurred where military use was so intense that joint operations with civilian users was no longer practical.

While DLAND investment in airport construction was substantial, and airports appropriated "for the duration" also made an important contribution, a significant number of new military airports were also built with military funding after America entered the war. As a result of all these efforts, by the war's end the country had gained a whopping 831 new airports rated Class IV or above (the highest ratings), and 484 airports rated Class III. This growth represented a 16-fold increase over the number of airports suitable for airline service before the war.

The new airports were badly needed during the war. The most pressing requirement was for training bases. In the four years following Pearl Harbor the country trained hundreds of thousands of air crew and used approximately 2,000 bases to do it.

The war also launched the biggest concentrated industrial expansion in America's history, which sent the demand soaring for airports. Domestic and international air transportation and freight operations became critically important to accomplish certain tasks with the urgency required by modern warfare. From requisitioning about 170 airliners at the outbreak of the war, the military air transport system grew in four years into an international airline operating thousands of aircraft on a network of routes spanning the globe.

The monumental volume of combat and support aircraft being produced also had to be handled on their way to the war. At the outbreak of hostilities there were approximately 350 airliners in the United States, practically all of them DC-3s. Within a couple of years America's airplane builders were flooding the globe with tens of thousands of aircraft. During the war the assembly lines churned out 12,000 more DC-3s, 13,000 Boeing B-17 and 18,000 Consolidated B-24 heavy bombers, thousands of fighters and training aircraft, and 1,700 four-engined DC-4 transports. Just to flight-test them and get them on their way to their ultimate destinations required that the military have access to hundreds of airports.

These military needs differed from the patterns of peacetime demand for air transportation and had an effect on the location of new airports that would have important postwar implications. While airfields were updated and established throughout the country, certain distinct regional patterns

25,000 a day!

Tremendous increases are foreseen in travel by air in the post-war era. Airports that can handle 25,000 passengers a day may be needed. Aluminum and magnesium will play a vital part in postwar aircraft and other products. Bohn engineers will be at your service in designing your products for use of these modern light alloys.

BOHN ALUMINUM AND BRASS CORPORATION
GENERAL OFFICES—LAFAYETTE BUILDING • DETROIT 26, MICHIGAN
Designers and Fabricators
ALUMINUM • MAGNESIUM • BRASS • AIRCRAFT-TYPE BEARINGS

BOHN

BUY
WAR
BONDS

This metal alloy manufacturer's advertisement at the end of World War II is remarkably prophetic of the shape of the modern airport to come. Its interpretation is reminiscent of Dallas/Fort Worth and Kansas City International, terminals that would be built in the 1970s. Note also the helicopters.

This advertisement's prediction proved utopian. Hoping to save the aviation industry's capacity in the postwar era, a prevailing view forecast a boom in private flying and predicted the need for hundreds of small sports-flying fields. A recession and a public belief that flying small aircraft was an unnecessary luxury put an end to such dreams, but the Cold War soon picked up the industrial slack.

emerged. Aircraft factory sites and the need for staging bases for overseas ferry flights led to the disproportionate location of airports on the East and West Coasts, and the fair-weather requirement for efficient flight training led to a heavy concentration of airports in the South.

The availability of a well developed airport infrastructure made an important contribution to the postwar transformation of the South and Southwest from predominantly agricultural or natural resource-based static communities into booming new economic frontiers. The ready-made network of mass air transportation was a factor in attracting new businesses and the economic migrants from the North to staff them. And as personal incomes recovered after the war and people had more money to spend on leisure time, it played an equally important role in transforming several of these areas, particularly Florida and the desert Southwest, into lucrative mass tourism destinations.

At war's end most airports taken over by the military "for the duration" were handed back to the civilian authorities, complete with improvements, which were quite a windfall.

Many military air bases constructed during the war were also turned over to the local authorities. The long list of large commercial airports which began life as air bases or airports built to support factories building military aircraft includes Chicago O'Hare; Bradley Field in Hartford, Connecticut; and Daytona Beach and Orlando, Florida. Many municipalities, including Tampa, Florida, and Detroit, Michigan, transferred their official airport from the smaller, less adequate municipal fields to the superior ex-military airports they inherited.

But dropping an airbase in the local town's lap wasn't always an ideal solution. Many of the bases were in out-of-the-way places, the locations of which had made military sense, but where there was little chance of attracting civilian air traffic. The towns that inherited them had a problem: The cost of maintaining the big, inherited bases could be prohibitive on limited, small-town municipal budgets. In a number of instances, closing the ex-bases was the only solution.

Some of the large, traditional urban centers had a different problem. When civilian traffic flows were reinstated and throngs of traveling businessmen took to the air with great postwar enthusiasm, the airports found their ground facilities struggling to keep pace with demand. The military hadn't been big on building passenger terminals and baggage handling facilities, and airports like Chicago, which had put expansion plans for terminals on hold for the war, faced overcrowding and customer complaints.

"Chicago is the worst," wrote a *Fortune* magazine writer in 1946. "Its airport is a slum. Chewing gum, orange peels, paper and cigar butts strew the floor around the stacks of luggage. One must line up even for the restrooms. The weary travelers sit or even lie on the floor. In such an atmosphere the beat-up traveler, interminably waiting for some unexplained reason, has no reason but to ponder bitterly on the brilliant ad that lured him with 'Travel with the Easy Swiftness of the Homeward Winging Birds.' "

This was the airlines' first brush with armies of irate passengers. The inadequacy of terminal space was compounded by a shortage of aircraft. Although the airport parking ramps were choking with ex-military transport aircraft, they couldn't be converted for civilian use fast enough to meet the surge in civilian demand.

These bottlenecks began to ease as the nation made the adjustment from a war footing to normal civilian life. The aircraft makers, eager for postwar work, accelerated their conversion programs, and were soon building new civilian airliners and planning bigger ones as America entered the Golden Age of the propliners.

The airports turned their attention to constructing new terminals or expanding existing ones, and the CAA concentrated on developing the postwar air transport system. It focused most of its attention on digesting navigation and communications technologies inherited from the war and applying them to improve and greatly expand the network of national airways.

The CAA also provided guidance for the establishment of the structure for postwar airport funding. The new rules were spelled out in the Federal Airport Act of 1946 after many hours of

cantankerous argument in Congress about its structure. Affirming the federal government's responsibility for a national air transportation system and recognizing the astronomical cost of building new airports and expanding existing ones, the Federal Airport Act established for the first time a funded program to aid airports.

It was called the Federal Aid Airport Program (FAAP) and authorized the spending of a half a billion dollars over seven years on airports. The program was to be managed by the CAA, but

Chicago's Midway Airport received a substantial airside upgrade during the war but had to put plans for a new terminal on hold. After the war a terminal was quickly built. It was a long, linear building, its monotony broken by three drum-shaped halls that gave Midway a characteristic appearance.

Right: New York's LaGuardia Airport was one of the busiest airports during the propliner era, handling the majority of New York City's scheduled domestic flights. Its original terminal eventually came under pressure from increasing traffic, and various gate extensions were built to cope until a new terminal could be built.

Congress had to authorize disbursals annually based on the CAA's recommendations.

The recipient local authority had to match FAAP funds, continuing the earlier relationship between federal and local funding. But a stubborn political struggle developed over the Act to decide whether the states or the municipalities would get the federal contribution and how it would be allocated geographically. Ultimately, the states ended up being responsible for about 75 percent of the disbursements, with individual shares determined by a formula based on the state's size and population. The CAA retained control over the remaining 25 percent of the funds at its own discretion.

FAAP was extended several times, although Congress proved more miserly with disbursements than was authorized, and the program lasted with modifications until it was replaced by the Airport and Airway Development Act of 1970.

At the end of the war the CAA and some members of Congress went through one last

Miami Airport, to the left, got a neighbor during World War II, a much larger army air base. Following the war the two fields were merged and have grown into Miami International Airport.

romantic infatuation with the vision of an airplane in every garage. In part, this view was motivated by the astonishingly massive role aviation had carved out for itself during the war. It wasn't unreasonable to imagine tens of thousands of pilots coming home to zip around the neighborhood in Piper Cubs and other small, inexpensive airplanes of their own.

Another reason to champion the small airplane's cause was somewhat more desperate. It was an attempt to salvage production capacity and jobs in an aircraft industry that was about to crash with the end of hostilities.

These views prompted the CAA once again to champion the cause of building small Class I and Class II airports. It was envisioned that 50 percent of the funds available under the Federal Airport Act would be spent on building such idyllic fields of flying.

In any the event, the idyll never materialized. In the relatively short but sharp recession that followed the war as the country struggled to readjust to a peacetime economy, small aircraft sales collapsed. When recovery came it did bring a robust general aviation industry that attracted its fair share of FAAP funds, but never on a scale envisioned by the last believers in an airplane in every garage.

What did materialize following the painful but relatively short postwar economic readjustment was the prosperity of the 1950s, a time of unprecedented national wellbeing that turned air travel from an expensive indulgence into just another form of mass transit.

As the propliner era got underway and passenger numbers soared, airports across the nation rushed to keep pace. Many had inherited vastly improved runway systems and technical facilities from the armed forces, but all had to focus on improving passenger-handling facilities.

Initially, many postwar terminals were functional, semi-permanent stopgap structures, little more than cinderblock corridors leading to simple, bare waiting rooms to provide shelter from the elements until it was time to walk out to the plane. As the number of passengers increased, these corridors and waiting pens spread like barnacles, gradually branching out from the main terminals. But soon they proved inadequate and began to give way to a crop of new, modern terminals built to make a statement and handle the masses.

ANOTHER PASSENGER SHOWS WHY AMERICAN SERVES YOU BETTER WHEN YOU FLY

"Nothing is too much for your Miss Jordan!"

It makes no difference to her how difficult or complicated the itinerary may be; she is always there with a smile, good humor and a willingness to serve. I, for one, like to go American because of people like Mary Jordan."

LEROY KING, NEW YORK CITY

Accurate attentive service with "the personal touch" is the trademark of American Airlines ticketing and reservations personnel. Whether answering questions, checking flight information or attending to your baggage, they are invariably as pleasant as they are precise. Equally responsible for the excellence of its service is American's record of constant pioneering in the development of new equipment. The newest facilities and finest personnel are good reasons why—whether you travel first class on the Mercury or the Captain's Flagship or aircoach on the Royal Coachman—American serves you better when you fly.

AA AMERICAN AIRLINES
America's Leading Airline

The ticketing agent at Midway, the nation's busiest airport in propliner days, could have her hands full at peak times as the skies became overcrowded and passenger dissatisfaction increased. Airline advertisements attempted to soothe ruffled passengers' sensibilities.

The biggest postwar airport project was instigated by a stocky little dynamo of a man famous for championing spectacular airports. In the spring of 1945 he was once again hammering home a visionary message to a captive audience on a vast strip of sandy Long Island marshland. They were looking at what was about to become the world's greatest airport, he told them with evangelical zeal.

He was Mayor Fiorello LaGuardia and he was championing a second airport for his beloved New York to a group of visiting fellow mayors. It would be ten times the size of the city's showcase airport that was named after him for his leading role in creating it, and it would cost an unprece-

SEATTLE-TACOMA AIRPORT
OWNED AND OPERATED BY THE PORT OF SEATTLE

dented $160 million. Its official name was to be New York International Airport, but from the beginning it would be known as Idlewild, after the surrounding neighborhood.

Many observers wondered why New York needed a second airport, let alone one so immense, but they lacked the mayor's shrewd foresight. LaGuardia extrapolated from developments in commercial aviation that international air travel would be the next big thing, and he was determined to secure New York's role as the world's gateway to the East Coast of America. From the rapid growth in air traffic at

nearby LaGuardia Airport, which had little room to expand, he knew that there was no such thing as an airport that was too large. Thus, LaGuardia connived to acquire 4,527 acres for his new project.

Idlewild started life as a marshy golf course and an adjacent turf landing strip for sport pilots. In 1942 it took the first steps toward turning into a major airport when it became one of the wartime airport development projects. But the task was so huge that by war's end it hadn't gotten beyond the landfill stage, which had already consumed $60 million. And therein Mayor LaGuardia saw his chance and

The Seattle-Tacoma Airport was one of many run by the Port Authority of the cities it served. Such airports benefited from professional management and were run on a profit basis, earning income from facility leases, user fees, and other sources.

rammed his proposal through the local and national approval process with characteristic determination.

Idlewild's development progressed smoothly, but when Mayor LaGuardia was succeeded by Mayor O'Dwyer in late 1945, its future came into serious doubt. The new mayor found it difficult to justify saddling the city with Idlewild's exorbitant cost, so he launched an effort to find alternative uses for the site. By 1946 he concluded that completing the airport would bring the city the most benefit after all, but it also made sense to get the city out of direct involvement in airport construction and operation.

To solve the problem, the Port of New York Authority, an organization highly experienced in developing and running a multimillion-dollar transportation facility, was asked to consider taking over direct responsibility for managing not only Idlewild, but also LaGuardia Airport. In June, 1947 the Port Authority signed a 50-year lease to run the airports, and the development of Idlewild could continue.

The Port Authority's takeover was a relatively early example of an airport management arrangement that was pioneered by Oakland Airport in 1927 and has since become a popular solution for cities to manage their airports. Among them are Boston's Logan Airport and Hanscom Field, run by the Port Authority of Massachusetts since 1955, and Seattle-Tacoma Airport in Washington state.

Idlewild opened on July 31, 1948, with a nine-day airshow and drew President Truman to make the opening speech. It resembled a large air base similar to many that had been built in the preceding years. It had a superb network of runways and navigation equipment capable of handling the largest, most modern aircraft, but its terminal and other buildings were minimal. A small, functional, WPA-style, one-story terminal designed by Delano and Aldrich was topped by a simple tower cab. Quonset huts stretching to the left and right provided additional space.

The passenger facilities may not have been much, but the sign above the airside terminal door said "New York International Airport", and the

A propliner climbs out of Cleveland Hopkins Airport on a rainy day. The National Air Races of the 1920s and '30s held at that site have long ago passed into history.

foreign airlines and America's designated international carriers flocked to it in droves. It made little economic sense for most foreign lines to fly to New York, but the city was the most prestigious place to show the national flag, and their governments willingly subsidized their losses. The handful of passengers they carried could be easily accommodated by the spartan facilities, and the Port Authority thought it could take its time to plan fancier accommodations for the anticipated growth in traffic.

The first passenger to step off a scheduled airliner at Idlewild was four-year-old Donna Moore, arriving from Santiago, Chile, on a Peruvian International Airlines DC-4. The exotic foreign logos soon to be glimpsed alongside the more familiar Pan American and TWA liveries included Air France, BOAC, Avianca, KLM, Iberia, FAMA Argentine Airlines, Trans Canada Airlines, Swissair, Sabena, El Al, SAS, and LAI, the forerunner of Alitalia.

While initially Idlewild was primarily an international gateway, National Airlines and Eastern Airlines provided early domestic service. In the next few years, regulators allowed most of the major domestic lines to join them.

In 1952 Sabena Belgian Airlines came up with a twist on the concept of no-frills coach class that had become increasingly popular since first introduced in 1948. In the beginning the classes flew separately. An airplane was configured either as all coach or all first class. Not having the resources to run all coach flights to the United States, Sabena introduced the mixed class service: part coach, part first class.

Other airlines in a similar situation were quick to follow suit. The good times of the 1950s were also just about beginning to roll. Suddenly, going by air to Europe became affordable, and the Port Authority found itself running out of time to provide the fancier passenger-handling facilities that were always Idlewild's due.

The Port Authority completed its master plan by 1955. It called for an oval-shaped terminal area at the center of the runway system on 650 acres of land. A circular road system would provide access. Ringing the oval, the major U.S. airlines and

Britain's BOAC would build showcase terminals. The complex of terminals was referred to as Terminal City. First among the terminals would be a lavish International Arrivals Building for the foreign airlines. Behind this building would be a new, eight-story control tower complex.

The International Arrivals Building was completed in 1957. Designed in International Style by the architectural firm of Skidmore, Owings, and Merrill, it gained critical acclaim and redefined the concept of the modern airline terminal. It was a vast, airy structure with unprecedented space, comfort, and amenities for passengers, and provisions for significant growth. The exterior was defined by the architects, but within the building each airline was free to design its own interior to imprint its own style on its passenger handling areas.

The building combined a linear main terminal with two finger pier terminals. Aircraft either taxied directly to the two wings extending to both sides of the main hall or to two finger extensions perpendicular to the hall. This layout was one of several terminal schemes that first appeared in the designs submitted for the Leigh Airports Competition in

Airline simulators began to play an important training role during the propliner era. Airports were ideal locations for these training centers. This simulator at Chicago's Midway Airport trains DC-6 pilots.

Travelers dressed for the occasion when they took an airline trip in the 1950s, whether they were traveling with friends, family or with an organized group. For most it was a special event, and many were also quite apprehensive.

1928 but weren't put into widespread use until after World War II.

A notable innovation of the arrivals building at Idlewild was the customs area. The customs examiners' stations were laid out in supermarket checkout counter style, capable of handling unprecedented volumes of arriving passengers. This layout was to become the standard at international airports in coming years.

Although arriving and departing passengers were vertically separated by two floors inside the terminal, the external passenger drop-off ramp and pick-up ramp were both at ground level. This arrangement would cause severe vehicular congestion in later years as passenger traffic approached the terminal's capacity limits.

Nearby Newark Airport in New Jersey, which closed after it lost out to newly opened LaGuardia in 1940, became a major transit base during the war for military aircraft being ferried to the various theaters of operation. It wound up with much improved runways and infrastructure. Following the war it was reopened as a civilian airfield, and the airlines who had deserted it for LaGuardia were enticed to return.

However, they found limited demand for their service under the strictly regulated routes they were allowed to serve in the New York area. The majority of passengers continued to prefer LaGuardia for domestic flights, and Idlewild had a monopoly on international flights.

In spite of this low demand, the city of Newark strongly preferred to have its own area airport but found it tough to meet the multimillion-dollar funding requirement for an airport's long-term development. Following the lead of New York City, Newark turned to the Port of New York Authority for help and found a positive reception. Newark joined LaGuardia and Idlewild under the Port Authority's management, an arrangement that continues today under the renamed Port Authority of New York and New Jersey. By 1952 Newark even boasted a new, modern passenger terminal—boxy, multilevel, and large—to take the pressure off the Art Deco gem of a terminal that trumped New York back in 1934.

A little over an hour's flight time up the coast from the New York area in an average propliner of

the 1950s, Boston's airport was filling out most of Boston Harbor to lay the foundations for its future role as a major international hub. Originally opened on 189 soggy acres, it had grown into an 1,800-acre airfield during the war with help from the armed forces. In the process, it had acquired a runway system that could easily handle any level of reasonably predictable demand and had plenty of room for further expansion.

By late 1949 the Boston airport got a new terminal, the Boutwell building. It was a large, simple, horseshoe shaped, centrally placed building that set the footprint for the airport's current layout of terminals and handled half a million passengers a year. Soon its various sections began to sprout finger piers for additional gates, and by 1955 it sported an eight-story tower, forerunner of the signature tower the airport received in the 1970s.

In 1955 the Massachusetts Legislature renamed the Boston airport the General Edward Lawrence Logan Airport, or Logan for short. General Logan was a veteran of the Spanish-American War of 1897 and a politician with a long list of local achievements but no recorded link to aviation. That same year the legislature formed the Port Authority of Massachusetts and placed Logan under its control along with the city's port facilities.

Massport, as the Port Authority is commonly known today, was given responsibility for Logan, to provide much needed professional management and dig it out of a multimillion-dollar deficit it had accumulated over the years. This was another example of a popular solution that emerged in the 1950s to deal with the increasing complexities and demands of airport management. By the time the propliner era approached its end in the late 1950s, Logan was

The Business Airport Business

There are over 5,300 airports open for public use in the United States, but the airlines provide service only to about 550 of them. Even the airports served by commercial airlines are often reachable only indirectly through connecting flights that can add hours to the trip. The national airport network gives businesses that can afford the use of private aircraft the opportunity to bypass the airlines and go directly to airports that are closest to their ultimate destinations.

There are plenty of companies that can foot the bill, so business aviation is big business. According to the National Business Aviation Association, in 2002 there were 9,709 companies operating 14,837 business aircraft in the United States. To put the number of business aircraft in perspective, the three largest airlines have fleets of approximately 300 aircraft each.

There is an acute need for comprehensive airport services for such a large number of business aircraft, which on average fly around 450 hours per year each. This demand has given rise to airport operators specializing in serving the business aviation community.

While there isn't such a thing as a business airport exclusively, in areas where business aviation activity is especially high there are airports whose primary function is to serve the business flyer. The ones near major airline hubs are commonly designated reliever airports. In the New York City area, Teterboro and Morristown airports in New Jersey, Westchester Airport in Westchester County, and Islip on Long Island are four favorites with business fliers. A few other examples of the thousands of such airports nationwide are

Houston Hobby, in Houston, Texas; Hanscom Field just west of Boston, Massachusetts; Burbank Airport in Burbank, California; Fort Lauderdale Executive in Fort Lauderdale, Florida; and Love Field in Dallas, Texas. These airports all have service businesses catering exclusively to business aviation, providing elegant transit lounges, crew rest and briefing facilities, fueling, maintenance services, hangarage, and even aircraft fleet management.

The experience of a machine tool maker in Hartford, who has a Cessna Citation business jet, provides a vivid example of the advantages of business flying over the airliners. In addition to his factory in Hartford, he also has a plant in Maine and likes to spend his weekends in his home in Florida. He can hop from

Hartford Brainard Airport, which is a few minutes from his factory, to a small airport near his plant in Maine in less than an hour in the Citation. By any alternate means of transportation the trip would take over half a day. Following the flight up from Hartford, on a Friday he can take off at the business day's end in Maine and be sitting down to a late dinner by 9:00 P.M. in Florida. And a dawn departure on Monday morning from Florida gets him back to Hartford by the start of the business day. Trying to do that on the airlines isn't a question of taking longer to get there. Without access to business airplanes and the thousands of airports that serve them, it would be impossible because it would take so long that it would be impractical.

A pair of Cessna Citations await their passengers at one of 4,500 airports in the United States accessible to business jets but not served by the airlines. In the foreground, the Citation VII rolls out the red carpet. In the background is a Citation X, which at a top speed of Mach .92 is the world's fastest business jet.

the nation's tenth busiest airport, handling over two million passengers a year.

Chicago Municipal Airport continued to be one of the nation's busiest during World War II. Its prewar plans to replace its simple, attractive International Style terminal that dated back to 1931 and had become woefully inadequate, were put on hold for the war's duration. Passenger traffic soared at Chicago Municipal in the war's aftermath, and construction of a new terminal became imperative. But its designer, the city's architect, Paul Gerhardt, who also designed the original terminal, faced a difficult challenge.

Chicago Municipal, renamed Midway in 1949 in honor of the World War II battle for the Pacific island, was hemmed in on all sides by development, with no prospect for further expansion. Yet, passengers continued to strongly prefer Midway because of its close proximity to downtown Chicago. Uncertain about the airport's future because of its limits to growth at a time of rapid expansion and technological progress in civil aviation, Gerhardt designed an attractive but inexpensive building.

It was an early example of the linear terminal, a long, narrow building facing the airport apron and receiving aircraft that taxied up to it side by side in a row. The architect broke up the length of the building with three visually pleasing, proportionally spaced, drum-shaped structures. The upper story of the central drum functioned as the air traffic control tower, and all three drums provided both landside and airside access.

Regrettably, the terminal's capacity was marginally adequate even as it opened in 1947. It handled passengers on a single ground-floor level and could serve only 15 aircraft at a time.

Notable at Midway were several graceful hangars built for American Airlines and TWA between 1948 and 1953. They were of pioneering thin-shell concrete construction. This new technique was not only pleasing to the eye, but yielded considerable savings on construction expenses. Similar techniques would soon be employed at other airports to build landmark passenger terminals.

Chicago's city officials recognized Midway's looming limitations as early as the mid 1940s and took steps to find an alternative solution. In 1946

Chicago acquired Orchard Field to the northwest of the city where the Douglas Aircraft Company had a plant making C-54s, the military version of the DC-4 during World War II. The city also had the foresight to acquire additional land in the next few years, bringing total acreage to over 7,000 acres.

Orchard Field already had a substantial airport built by Douglas, but it paled in comparison to what the city had in mind for its new airport to wean travelers away from convenient but congested Midway.

In 1949 Orchard Field was renamed Chicago O'Hare International Airport after naval aviator and Chicago native, Lt. Edward O'Hare, who died in combat in 1942 and won the Congressional Medal of Honor.

O'Hare's planning got underway in the late 1940s. By the early 1950s it was open to limited traffic, relying largely on the Douglas heritage, but it would take until 1963 and the jet age to complete the main terminal and convince the scheduled airliners to make the move from Midway.

At the end of World War II, Chicago got another airport, Meigs Field on the city's famed

TWA's elegant, spacious ticket office in Chicago in the 1950s impresses customers with the airline's global reach prominently displayed on the wall map.

Leinweber, a young architectural firm that would go on to become a major global force in airport design. Their terminal was a linear set of modular cross-vaulted halls of thin-shell concrete. The sides were huge, arched walls of glass that flooded the interior with natural light. Finger piers containing the passenger boarding gates extended from the vaulted halls.

The Lambert Field terminal could be easily extended by the addition of modular halls at both ends. On the landside it separated arriving and departing passengers on different levels. In many ways this terminal was a precursor of terminal design in the 1960s.

Kansas City got a new airport in the mid 1950s even though it didn't want one. Its old airport was very convenient to downtown, on a sharp bend of the Missouri River, but was getting a bit over-crowded without much room to expand. It was home base for TWA, which also had its main maintenance base there. In 1951 the river overflowed and flooded the airport, particularly wreaking havoc with TWA. The airline contemplated leaving altogether, but decided instead to move north of the city to an airport to be built. The new field, Kansas City International Airport, was opened in 1957 with an 8,000-foot runway and a big TWA maintenance facility. But all the airlines remained at the downtown airport as long as they could, not moving to KCI until 1972.

Across the continent on the Pacific coast, civil aviation was also quick to grow in the aftermath of World War II. By 1949 San Francisco Airport alone handled a million passengers a year, and by 1953 that figure had increased to two million. The growth in passengers was too much for its Spanish Revival terminal, which had been such a progressive building when it opened in 1937. It was time to take the next step, to develop a long-range master plan centered around a new, modern terminal.

It was also time to make a slight adjustment to the airport's name. As Pan American's landplanes took over from the last flying boats and headed for distant Pacific destinations, and foreign airlines, including British Commonwealth Pacific, Philippine Airlines, and China National Airways, began to appear on the routes established by landplanes during World War II,

This exotic tower at Phoenix Sky Harbor Airport in 1952 was one of the first attempts at making the tower a personal statement about an airport. Later, the FAA designed a standard tower which ensured consistency and efficiency but could be finished to any aesthetic design.

lakefront parkland. It was built on Northerly Island on the site of the 1933 World's Fair. No airport could have been more convenient for downtown, and it quickly became a favorite of business fliers. It was on prime real estate, though, and eventually it came under tremendous pressure from developers. As of 2003, the developers were winning.

In St. Louis, Missouri, Lambert Field benefited from one of the best-received new terminals of the 1950s. It was designed by Hellmuth, Yamasaki, and

This is an original china plate from the 500-seat restaurant at the Pittsburgh Airport's terminal in the 1950s. It features an image of the terminal, which looked back to the style of the 1930s but was one of the most spacious, up-to-date terminals of its time.

the former Mills Field became San Francisco International Airport, "Gateway to the Pacific."

San Francisco's new terminal—a sleek structure of reinforced concrete, steel, and glass—was strategically placed at the tip of a large oval driveway near the main access road and the intersection of its bisecting runways. It separated passenger flow vertically. Passengers arrived on the ground floor and exited on the same floor to a pickup section of the circular roadway. Departing passengers were dropped off on a separate upper roadway and entered the terminal on the upper floor to check in and proceed to the gates. Two radial finger piers jutted onto the tarmac on the terminal's airside to maximize the number of gates.

The finger piers heralded an option for the airport's aggressive expansion in coming years. A maze of terminals would eventually fully encircle the loop defined by the roadway and would also jut out onto the tarmac in the form of pier satellite terminals, linear terminals, and finger pier terminals.

Oakland Airport, San Francisco's rival across the bay, also took the propliner era in stride. It drew up an ambitious expansion plan which took over a

As the airline industry grew, the need for larger-capacity hangars became as pressing a need as that for bigger passenger terminals. United Airlines' hangar at San Francisco Airport, completed in 1958, was considered an impressive engineering achievement for its wide-span beams and elegant design. When completed it could accommodate two of the company's new Douglas DC-8 jetliners.

decade to complete, and found a new niche as one of the most important West Coast terminals for a new type of carrier, the charter operator.

Known as non-scheduled airlines, or non-scheds for short, charter operators experienced explosive growth after the war. They played a leading role in bringing cheap air travel to the masses. Key to their success was the availability of surplus military transports which they converted into civilian airliners. They crammed them as full as possible with the narrowest practical seats and sent them on their way when all the seats were sold. Tickets went for a fraction of the ticket price for the same trip on a scheduled flight. For $99 they would take their passengers from coast to coast.

Charter operators were able to get around the strict regulation of airline routes that rationed the amount of service and controlled ticket prices because they were not flying on fixed schedules. They theoretically provided only occasional services to ad hoc destinations, so the rules didn't apply to them.

Initially not known for the highest maintenance standards and reliability on their shoestring budgets, and often flying at odd hours, they gave rise to the term "fly-by-night operator." But while economically they were risky businesses, they proved to be safer than their reputation suggested and gave valuable business to the secondary airports they favored which were neglected or bypassed by the airlines, such as Oakland and Newark.

The postwar years also brought big changes to the airports of the Los Angeles area, home to one of the highest concentrations of the country's aviation industry. The Douglas Aircraft Company, Lockheed, and others had expanded exponentially during the war, as did the associated airports. By the war's end Los Angeles Municipal Airport stood to gain the most for one simple reason: It was surrounded by thousands of acres of farm land, unlike Burbank, the prewar airport that still had the majority of the airline traffic but was now owned by Lockheed and was the site of its main plant, and Glendale, the other popular civilian field.

Los Angeles Municipal had been home to important aircraft plants for Douglas, Northrop, and North American since the 1930s. It was also a key aircraft transit base during the war and had grown to 2,500 acres by the end of 1945. Its runways were substantially expanded and lengthened, setting up the beginnings of the present parallel runway configuration. A row of temporary, one-story passenger terminals was constructed, and the airport was back in the civilian aviation business full time.

It didn't take long for the airlines to anticipate Los Angeles Municipal's promising future. By 1947 it had become the city's premiere airport for scheduled airline services, and it has never looked back. New services were established as the airlines expanded, and existing operations were transferred from Burbank Airport, which became one of Los Angeles' most important general and business aviation fields in addition to continuing to serve Lockheed.

The Los Angeles Department of Airports produced its first master plan in 1946, calling for further extension of the runways and the establishment of a terminal infrastructure. In 1949 the airport was renamed Los Angeles International Airport. During the 1950s the runways were further expanded, and the airport rapidly became one of the busiest in the nation. Vehicular congestion became a major problem, but the long row of functional, simple terminals, built barely to strip mall standards, managed to cope with the growing traffic and were destined to serve into the beginnings of the jet age.

The most glamorous airline destination in America and its territories was not on the West Coast but 2,400 miles further west. It was Honolulu, Hawaii, and the age of the propliner opened it up to the new era of mass tourism. Prior to the war, only a handful of Pan American's flying boats served Hawaii by air. Passenger capacity was limited by the small size of Pan Am's fleet, and the cost of the tickets was astronomical. Only the super-rich could afford to go to Hawaii by air, or had the time to go by sea. But the big, mass-produced, four-engined landplanes of World War II made crossing the Pacific routine, and their civilian successors made Hawaii accessible and affordable to the merely well-to-do.

When the fleets of propliners appeared on the eastern horizon bearing full loads of well-off tourists, Honolulu's John Rogers Airport, founded in 1927, was ready for them. It had three long runways built

This aerial survey shot of Chicago's Midway Airport shows that it was completely hemmed in by its neighborhood, making any runway expansion impossible. This situation required a second airport for Chicago, which it got with the development of O'Hare.

The new terminal at St. Louis Airport, designed by Hellmuth, Yamasaki, and Leinweber and completed in 1956, received rave reviews. Its thin-shell modular construction allowed for expansion at both ends of the completed sections by the addition of more modules.

by the military in 1943 to handle the large volume of transpacific traffic during the war. They were built on landfill sourced by dredging the adjacent Keehi Lagoon, which got an expanded seaplane base.

In 1947 the John Rogers Airport was given the more recognizable name of Honolulu Airport. Two years later it got one of the longest runways in the world. A connecting link was paved to Hickam Air Force Base next door, giving the two fields a joint 13,000-foot runway. This was more important to the military's heavily laden, long-range strategic jet bombers coming into service than the civilian propliners using Honolulu Airport.

As the demand for air service to Honolulu surged after the war, the regulators permitted first United and then Northwest Orient and others to join Pan American in serving the islands. When the big, luxurious Boeing Stratocruisers entered service starting in 1949, they became the favored airliners on the prestige route and were seen daily at Honolulu in different liveries until the advent of the jets. For a time the Stratocruiser's aft honeymoon suite offered by several airliners was a coveted spot for couples on a dream vacation making the 10-hour crossing from the mainland.

Tourism accounted for an increasing share of the rapid growth in airline service throughout the country, but nowhere as dramatically as in Florida. In fact, the airlines made Florida a year-round destination when they made an agreement with the hotel operators to fly full, year-round schedules if the hotels remained open throughout the year.

Eastern Airlines dominated this growing north-south market along the East Coast. It was followed by feisty Miami-based National, which expanded rapidly to serve the Southeast from New York when allowed to do so by the regulators after the war. And the Florida tourist market was in large part responsible for transforming Delta Airlines into a major regional airline, especially following its merger with Chicago and Southern Airlines.

When the airlines were ready to descend on Florida with increasing planeloads of tourists by the late 1940s, Florida's airports were ready to receive them. Because of its favorable weather and strategic southeastern location, Florida was one of the states that benefited the most from the construction of air bases during World War II. Although many of the larger cities and towns had established airports in the 1920s and 1930s, they paled in comparison to the bases inherited after the war.

Miami Airport at 36th Street, built by Pan American, was dwarfed by the Miami Army Airfield constructed adjacent to it by the Corps of Engineers. As many as 114,000 pilots were trained at the army airfield at the height of the war, and the Port Authority of Miami acquired it in 1947. In 1949 the Port Authority rerouted the Seaboard Railroad tracks that separated the two airports and renamed the united facility Miami International Airport just in time for the airlines' agreement with the hoteliers to keep the hotels open year round.

Other Florida communities whose present-day airports started as wartime military bases or were greatly enlarged during the war include Orlando, Daytona Beach, Boca Raton, Melbourne, Fort Myers, and Fort Lauderdale. Tampa switched scheduled airline service from its prewar field, Peter O. Knight Airport, to Drew Field, which the military built and used to train 125,000 air crew during the war. Drew Field is Tampa International Airport today.

Palm Beach, one of the most exclusive prewar winter retreats for the rich, had to fight for its airport, Morrison Field, with the military during the 1950s. The field had become a major Air Transport Command base during World War II, and was turned over to the county in 1947. A year later, county officials changed its name to Palm Beach International Airport in anticipation of the growth to come.

All was well until 1951, when the Air Force reactivated the airport as a military training base for the Korean War. The town's patriotic residents had no problem with this identity change and were appropriately supportive of the 23,000 airmen trained there. But they objected strenuously when, after the war, the Air Force attempted to make the field a permanent military air base, which would have forced the community to share it at the expense of civilian growth. The county had to battle with the federal government until 1959 to get its airport back.

Other important airports of the propliner era included Atlanta's Hartsfield Airport, Houston Hobby, Dallas Love Field, Minneapolis-St. Paul, Cleveland Hopkins, Denver Stapleton, Seattle-Tacoma, McCarran Airport in Las Vegas, and San Diego's Lindbergh Field. They all expanded significantly along similar lines, improving both their runway systems and terminal facilities. Along with so many other airports, they became the fabric of the national air transportation system that was first

envisioned in the 1930s and became a reality in the 1950s.

In 1956 tragedy led to another important development of the national airport and airway system. On a bright, partly cloudy day over the Grand Canyon, a TWA Constellation and a United DC-7, both eastbound, collided when one of the airplanes changed altitude. All 127 passengers on the two airplanes died. Under the air traffic control system in place, the airliners' crews were responsible for maintaining separation from one another, and the system broke down.

As a result of this accident the air traffic rules changed. Aircraft under instrument flight plans were put strictly under the air traffic controllers' direction. It became the controllers' responsibility to maintain separation between aircraft under such flight plans. The government also embarked on an urgent program of equipping the airway system with more and better radar equipment to help the controllers.

The Grand Canyon accident and other safety problems with the airway system also led to the

This interior view of the St. Louis terminal shows it full of light and indicates the easy expansion potential at the end of the terminal.

A TWA Constellation takes on catering supplies for another long transatlantic flight. Catering was big business at airports. Several airlines established flight kitchens at their main bases which did a lucrative sideline provisioning other airlines that did not have their own facilities.

transformation of the CAA. The Federal Aviation Act of 1958 created the Federal Aviation Agency, which assumed the responsibilities of the CAA and was finally made independent of the Department of Commerce. By 1972, the FAA had become the Federal Aviation Administration and merged into the Department of Transportation, which is the structure that continues today.

The airports had expanded swiftly to cater to the propliner during the 1950s, but there were signs that they were about to be severely challenged again. When San Francisco's new terminal was completed in 1954, the airport staged a grand opening attended by the usual contingent of VIPs and thousands of ordinary citizens. It was a perfect California day and they crowded the terminal's spacious balcony built especially for spectators.

They admired Pan American's Boeing Stratocruiser, so popular on the run to Honolulu, and American's Douglas DC-7C, the first airliner able to reliably cross the United States nonstop against prevailing winds. However, what most caught their attention was a sparkling military airplane with sharply swept wings. It was about as big as the propliners but much sleeker, with narrow engine pods slung under its wings and no propellers. It was a Boeing B-47 Stratojet, America's first jet bomber, and it could go over twice as fast as the state-of-the-art civilian propliners parked next to it.

The B-47 on the ramp that day was an early warning that the propliners would soon be obsolete. Within a few years they would be superseded by America's first civilian jetliners, the Boeing 707 and the Douglas DC-8. The jets' speed and efficiency, later combined with airline deregulation, would trigger an exponential expansion in air travel that would push the nation's airport infrastructure to its limits and redefine the concept of the modern airport.

Chapter Five
New Cathedrals

When Captain Hamilton Smith of American Airlines started flying the first Boeing 707 jets, he loved streaking across the continent twice as fast as the DC-7 propliner he used to fly, but he earned his flight pay on the departures. "Every takeoff was marginal," he recalled to journalist Carl Solberg. "We used every available foot of runway. At San Francisco the landing gear would sometimes hit the localizer shack lifting off the end of the runway."

Relative to later models, the early jets were underpowered, which made little difference at their cruising altitudes, but required such long takeoff runs that they were unable to use many of the nation's existing runways. Often, weather conditions even restricted them from taking off on the runways open to them. Many early jet passengers who eagerly anticipated a smooth, swift trip were disappointed when their flight had to be cancelled because the outside air temperature was too high to allow the engines to crank out sufficient thrust for takeoff.

The early Boeing 707s were known as water wagons because they carried gallons of water to pour into their engines to increase their anemic thrust during the takeoff roll. The water turned into steam, enriching the air and enabling the fuel to burn with greater intensity and release more energy. It was a

The barrel-vaulted American Airlines terminal at Chicago O'Hare lets in as much natural light as possible, and it is thoughtfully decorated in soothing tones to minimize the stress of peak-time air travel.

Oakland airport enters the jet age with a new terminal and a new arrival from distant Europe, parked under the wing of a member of the old guard.

stopgap measure that turned every takeoff into an airshow act, as long plumes of sooty steam billowed out of the engines and spectators held their breath to see if the thundering jet would stagger into the air by the runway's end.

More powerful engines soon toned down the drama. Improved, high-lift wing designs also shortened takeoff distances, but neither development was enough to do away with the need for longer and more runways to handle the jets.

And it wasn't just the runways. The jets' stellar speed and efficiency severely challenged the entire civil aviation infrastructure. The Boeing 707 and Douglas DC-8 were twice as fast as the DC-7 and Lockheed Constellation propliners and carried almost twice as many passengers. And, to the greatest surprise of industry experts, the smooth jet engines of the 707 and DC-8 proved to be far more reliable than the propliners' cantankerous, failure-prone piston engines. They required much less routine care and were capable of running for thousands of hours longer between overhauls.

All these factors added up to much greater productivity. By the time a Lockheed Constellation plodded across the continent from Los Angeles to New York with 80 passengers, a 707 had delivered 140 passengers in half the time and was half way back to Los Angeles with 140 more on the return trip. As the jets forced out the propliners, more passengers were flying faster and more frequently than ever.

In 1958 when the first U.S. jets entered service in insignificant numbers, the airlines flew 34 billion passenger miles. In 1963, the first year that jets were in the fleet in significant numbers, the total passenger miles flown were 55 billion. This kind of growth soon set off a boom in airport expansion. Runways were extended and strengthened, new ones were built, new terminals rose next to them, and even entire new jetports were constructed.

The air terminal that most caught the popular attention at the dawn of the jet age was TWA's futuristic new building at New York's Idlewild Airport, opened in May 1962. Created by Finnish architect Eero Saarinen, it was a swirling, flowing

Dulles International Airport, Washington, D.C.'s second airport, was America's first civilian airport specifically built to be a jetport. Dulles was needed because the capital of the world's most powerful country found itself in the embarrassing position of not having an airport capable of dispatching jets to Europe and other long-distance international destinations.

Below: Eero Saarinen's terminal at Washington Dulles is a masterpiece of lightness in concrete and glass. The concrete roof seems to levitate on walls of glass. It is all achieved by clever structural engineering.

tribute in thin-shell concrete to the spirit of flight. Some said Saarinen was inspired by playing around with the hollow rind of half a grapefruit he'd finished at breakfast one morning, but the architect denied having been directly influenced by any physical object to create his abstract design.

The structure resembles two billowing wings about to lift off. Inside, natural light streaming in through glass walls and long, narrow openings in the ceiling illuminated the soaring, curving interior in an ever-changing pattern of light. Imaginative passengers with time on their hands could get the impression of already being aloft within a canyon of clouds, especially when the light was just right. The Jetsons would have felt right at home.

The main color of note was TWA's red, in various accent stripes, on signage, lettering, and logo displays, in an early example of modern corporate branding that was gaining popularity.

In its functional layout the terminal was more old fashioned than its appearance revealed. It was horizontally divided, with ticketing under one wing

and baggage claim under the other, accessed from the landside by a single-level driveway. Two piers led from the central hall to satellite boarding gates.

Ironically, while it looked more futuristic than most terminal designs to this day, the TWA

Chicago's O'Hare Airport was just what the city needed to replace hemmed-in, restricted Midway as the city's primary airport. The airy "glass cage" terminal was completed in 1963, just in time for the new jets. The banks of chairs designed by Charles Eames have since become classic.

terminal was designed for propliners. Commissioned in 1956, long before TWA's eccentric owner, Howard Hughes, had made any commitment to jets, the terminal's ergonomics and size were tailored to serving the airline's Constellations and the volume of passengers they carried. As a result, the terminal was only marginally adequate on opening day, and with little room to expand it would remain functionally problematic to the end of TWA's days.

The TWA terminal's jet-age appearance, not inspired by the jets, is instructive. Saarinen, who sadly passed away nine months before completion of the TWA terminal, gave his imagination free reign to express the ideal of flight in his mind. The modern jets, with their form following their function out of necessity more strictly than most human creations, came closer than any other aircraft to expressing the ideal of flight. Thus, when they arrived, they fit in with Saarinen's terminal far more naturally than any propliner.

Several spots away on the necklace of terminals that constituted Idlewild's growing Terminal City, on the other side of the International Arrivals Building, rose the Pan American terminal. Pan Am was America's premiere international airline, and Idlewild was its most prestigious base. Completed in 1963, Pan Am's terminal became another landmark for frequent international air travelers.

The original Pan Am terminal was a striking circular glass and concrete structure featuring an upper departure floor and a lower arrival floor. It had a large, overhanging concrete roof that provided protection from the elements prior to the introduction of jetways. A larger, triangular extension was later added which reached beyond the original building onto the tarmac and greatly increased the number of Pan Am's gates.

While an attractive structure, Pan Am's terminal was most remembered for what it represented.

An aerial view of Chicago O'Hare's terminal complex shortly after it was opened. The round building is a restaurant. Later a massive hotel and tower would rise on the oval space between the terminal and the parking lot. Note the propliners and jets on the ramp and the blissfully light traffic compared to today.

Dallas/Fort Worth nears completion in the early 1970s. Decades of wrangling between the two cities about a joint airport enabled them to build the world's biggest jetport for its day when they were finally forced into an agreement by the FAA.

The inter-terminal train at Dallas/Fort Worth was a joint first use of this mode of transportation, concurrently with Tampa airport's similar system.

Today we are used to the idea of the airlines linking any major airport with all corners of the world. But in the 1960s it was a special thrill just to see Pan Am's arrivals and departure board and realize that a single airline served such far-flung destinations as Nairobi, Delhi, Cairo, Beirut, Johannesburg, Tokyo, Caracas, Rio de Janeiro, and Buenos Aires, beyond the more familiar places like London, Frankfurt, Madrid, and Rome.

A sad but important moment in Idlewild's history took place on Christmas Eve, 1963. On that date the airport was renamed John F. Kennedy International Airport and became known as JFK in remembrance of the President who was assassinated in November of that year.

A few miles to the north of JFK, LaGuardia was having a hard time with the jet age in the early

Newark Airport's new terminal complex, completed in 1973, provides an attractive external façade. The problem with these cavernous new concrete palaces could be a poor, drab interior finish that achieved nothing with the space provided.

1960s. Similar to many other important airports throughout the country, its 5,000-foot runways were too short to handle jetliners. LaGuardia needed an extra 1,000 feet just to accommodate the smaller, regional Boeing 727 that was on the drawing board and would become a mainstay of the domestic airline industry. Unlike most other airports, LaGuardia had little room for expansion. Undaunted, the airport pressed ahead. It constructed two piers right into Flushing Bay and pushed the length of both its runways to 7,000 feet.

LaGuardia also got a new modern glass and concrete terminal, seven times the size of Delano and Aldrich's Art Deco gem that it replaced. A new 12-story vase-shaped control tower rose in front of the new terminal, one of the first towers in the country that sought to make an aesthetic statement. LaGuardia even fought off one of the first large-scale neighborhood revolts—another sign of coming times—that wished to restrict the noisy jets to nearby JFK. All of the improvements were completed by 1964, in time for LaGuardia's 25th anniversary and the arrival of the first Boeing 727s.

Washington, D.C., was slow to get a suitable airport back in the 1930s, and almost as soon as Washington National was ready in 1940, the authorities began considering the possibility of an additional airport for the capital. Discussions about a second airport dragged on into the 1950s, bogging down frequently in political gamesmanship. In the meantime, National was becoming congested, and it was becoming increasingly clear that it would only be partially adequate for the coming jet age. Particularly embarrassing was the looming prospect that the capital city of the world's most powerful country would not be able to launch nonstop transatlantic jet flights to Europe for the want of an airport.

Finally, in 1958 President Eisenhower personally intervened to gain agreement for locating the new airport in Chantilly, Virginia. A consortium including architect Eero Saarinen was assembled to develop the new field, and the design of Dulles International Airport got underway.

Dulles was the first airport explicitly designed for jets. Located on 10,000 acres, it set a new standard for the modern jetport. Its two parallel runways are 11,500 feet long, and a crosswind runway is 10,000 feet in length. Its terminal is strategically located between the two runways, a configuration that would become popular at successive jetports.

The terminal is another masterpiece by Saarinen that achieves a sense of lightness with an imposing mass of glass and concrete. The massive, inwardly curved concrete roof looks as if it is floating on a glass rectangle. The building's interior is a single, unobstructed hall that can be configured and reconfigured in any way desired.

The control tower is an integral part of the terminal complex. Placed on the tarmac in front of the terminal, it provides vertical balance to the horizontal terminal building to achieve a sense of equilibrium.

Eero Saarinen's personal expression of flight in his design of JFK's TWA terminal happily coexisted with the aeronautical engineer's functional design of the most suitable form for a passenger jet.

Below: Pan American's terminal at JFK is seen here at night, when most of its flights to Europe and Latin America have left. Metal sculptures of the signs of the zodiac adorn the departure-level driveway. The signs represent the constellations by which Pan American pilots navigated at night around the globe in the early days.

The vast size of Dulles required a creative solution to boarding aircraft distant from the terminal in a timely fashion. The problem was solved with the first use of mobile lounges built specially for Dulles by the Chrysler Corporation. The lounges are bus-like vehicles that can rise to be flush with the aircraft door. Passengers board the lounge at the terminal. The lounge sinks to ground level and is driven to the aircraft like a bus. It then rises to the aircraft door level and the passengers board directly, stepping from the lounge straight into the aircraft. This is a faster option to using buses and keeps passengers entirely out of the elements.

Dulles was planned to permit substantial expansion through the construction of remote terminals between the runways. Four remote terminals have been built so far. They are simple linear terminals with access to the aircraft via jetways. Mobile lounges transport the passengers between the main and remote terminals. In the most recent expansion plan of Dulles there are provisions for

constructing an inter-terminal rail system that has become an excellent mode of connecting terminals at other jetports.

Dulles opened to great critical acclaim in 1962, but was underutilized for many years. In its first year it handled only 50,000 passengers. Travelers preferred National because it was only four miles from downtown. Also, by the mid 1960s several medium-range jets had entered service which could use National, giving it a new lease on life in the jet age. Later a new generation of heavier jets with high-lift wings was also able to use National, further extending the airport's popularity. As the sheer volume of air traffic rose, by the 1980s Dulles also rose to its potential. Today, Dulles handles 13 million passengers per year, with plenty of room for further expansion.

The arrival of the jet age was also the making of Chicago's O'Hare International Airport. Travelers continued to favor cramped, crowded Midway throughout the 1950s because of its close proximity to the city, in spite of the availability of O'Hare's more distant wide-open spaces from 1955.

In 1959 Midway served 10 million passengers compared to only 2 million passing through O'Hare. But by 1962 all the scheduled airlines had moved to O'Hare. Midway's one square mile of space, completely surrounded by city blocks, could no longer compete with O'Hare's five runways suitable for jets, including one that was 13,000 feet long.

But there was still life for Midway after being abandoned by the scheduled airlines. It began to cater to the more upscale businessmen, those with their own planes. Its closeness to the city continued to be highly prized, and it became one of the nation's busiest business airports. And after the deregulation of the airlines in 1978, Midway would make one of the most remarkable comebacks as a major airport for scheduled carriers.

The planning of O'Hare was undertaken soon after World War II by Chicago's recently retired city civil engineer, Ralph Burke. He envisioned a cluster

Pan American's administrative building at Miami International Airport is constructed in a style matching that of several U.S. embassies built around the world at the same time. It is a revealing symbol of Juan Trippe's view of Pan American's role as America's representative to the world.

of Y-shaped buildings in the center of a runway system that radiated outward, similar to the spokes of a wheel. Burke's master plan was completed in 1952. Construction progressed slowly, but in 1956 Burke passed away. His role was assumed by the firm of C. F. Murphy Associates, who comprehensively revised the master plan for the coming jet age.

In spite of the substantial changes to bring the plans up to date for jet aircraft, the new architects respected the spirit of the original design, and in 1963 O'Hare at last got its Modern Style smoked glass and concrete terminal. It was segmented into three interconnected buildings, each with finger piers that contained the gates. O'Hare's gates were among the first to be equipped with jetways for boarding the aircraft. Passenger circulation was accommodated on two levels, with arrivals downstairs and departures upstairs. A circular restaurant building accommodated people with time on their hands and a desire for a little more ambience than the passenger waiting areas.

The spacious terminal's steel-framed glass walls invited the visual exploration of the outside. Charles Eames, an industrial designer working for Herman Miller, created inviting, ergonomically designed seats for the upper departure area. That style of seats became widely used at airports throughout the world and has become a design icon.

Kansas City Airport had served as TWA's maintenance base since the late 1950s and became the city's primary airport when the terminal complex was completed in 1972.

Airport Numbers and Types

There were 19,306 airports in the United States as of the 100th anniversary of flight. Of these airports, 5,314 were open to the public. The others were mostly small private strips for their owners' amusement. Of the airports open to the public, 4,160 were publicly owned and 1,154 were in private hands. Of the airports open to the public, 3,364 qualified to be included in the National Plan for Integrated Airport Systems (NPIAS). Here's how the FAA further defines them:

Commercial Service Airports

Commercial service airports are defined as public airports receiving scheduled passenger service and having 2,500 or more enplaned passengers per year. There are 546 commercial service airports. Of these, 422 have more than 10,000 enplanements and are classified as primary airports.

Primary airports receive an annual apportionment of at least $1 million in AIP funds (when AIP funding levels meet or exceed $3.2 billion), with the amount determined by the number of enplaned passengers.

Large Hubs

The term "hub" is used by the FAA to identify very busy commercial service airports. For instance, large hubs are those airports that each account for at least one percent of total U.S. passenger enplanements. Some enplanements originate in the local community and some consist of en route passengers transferring from one flight to another. Several large hub airports have little passenger transfer activity (Fort Lauderdale, Tampa, Boston, LaGuardia, Ronald Reagan Washington National, and San Diego International, for example), while transfers account for more than half of the traffic at others

(Cincinnati, Atlanta, Pittsburgh, St. Louis, and Dallas/Ft. Worth, for example). Together the 31 large hub airports account for 70 percent of all passenger enplanements. Large hub airports tend to concentrate on airline passenger and freight operations and have limited general aviation activity. Five large hub airports (Salt Lake City, Honolulu, Las Vegas, Miami, and Phoenix) have an average of 350 based aircraft, but the other 26 large hubs average only 39 based aircraft each. Thus, locally based general aviation plays a relatively small role at most large hubs.

The Nation's air traffic delay problems are concentrated at 31 large hub airports where the average delay per aircraft operation was 6.14 minutes in 2000. Delays occur primarily during instrument weather conditions when runway capacity is reduced below that needed to accommodate airline schedules.

Medium Hubs

Medium hubs are defined as airports that each account for between 0.25 percent and 1 percent of the total passenger enplanements. There

Boston Logan in 1924 (top) and in 1984 (bottom).

DISTRIBUTION OF ACTIVITY

Number Airports	Airport Type	Percentage of All Enplanements	Percentage of Active GA Aircraft *
31	Large-Hub Primary	69.6	1.3
37	Medium-Hub Primary	19.3	2.9
74	Small-Hub Primary	7.7	4.7
280	Nonhub Primary	3.2	11.3
124	Other Commercial Service	0.1	2.0
260	Relievers	0.0	27.1
2,558	General Aviation	0.0	37.2
3,364	Total Existing NPIAS Airports	100.0	86.4
15,942	Other Low Activity Landing Areas (Non-NPIAS)	0.0	13.6

* Based on active aircraft fleet of 219,464 aircraft in 1999.

are 37 medium hub airports, and together they account for 19 percent of all enplanements. Medium hub airports usually have sufficient capacity to accommodate air carrier operations and a substantial amount of general aviation. Medium hub airports have an average of 169 based aircraft. The delay per operation averaged 3.2 minutes for the 37 medium hub airports in 2000.

Small Hubs

Small hubs are defined as airports that each enplane 0.05 percent to 0.25 percent of the total passenger enplanements. There are 74 small hub airports that together account for 8 percent of all enplanements. Less than 25 percent of the runway capacity at small hub airports is used by airline operations, so these airports can accommodate a great deal of general aviation activity, with an average of 139 based aircraft. These airports are typically uncongested and do not account for significant air traffic delays.

Nonhub Primary

Commercial service airports that enplane less than 0.05 percent of all commercial passenger enplanements but more than 10,000 annually are categorized as nonhub primary airports. There are 280 nonhub primary airports that together account for 3 percent of all enplanements. These airports are heavily used by general aviation aircraft, with an average of 89 based aircraft.

Other Commercial Service

Commercial service airports enplaning 2,500 to 10,000 passengers annually are categorized as other commercial service airports. There are 124 of these airports in the NPIAS, and they account for 0.1 percent of all enplanements. These airports are used mainly by general aviation and have an average of 36 based aircraft.

Reliever Airports

General aviation pilots often find it difficult and expensive to gain access to congested airports, particularly large and medium hub airports. In recognition of this, the FAA has encouraged the development of high capacity general aviation airports in major metropolitan areas. These specialized airports, called relievers, provide pilots with attractive alternatives to using congested hub airports. They also provide general aviation access to the surrounding area. The 260 reliever airports have an average of 228 based aircraft, and together account for 27 percent of the Nation's general aviation fleet. All of the airports that are designated as relievers by the FAA are included in the NPIAS.

General Aviation Airports

Communities that do not receive scheduled commercial service may be included in the NPIAS as sites for general aviation airports if they account for enough activity (usually at least 10 locally owned aircraft) and are at least 20 miles from the nearest NPIAS airport. The activity criterion may be relaxed for

1038 Cheyenne Transcontinental Airport, Wyoming

Cheyenne (Wyoming) Airport in 1931 (top) and in 2001(bottom).

remote locations or other mitigating circumstances. The 2,558 general aviation airports in the NPIAS tend to be distributed on a one-per-county basis in rural areas and are often located near the county seat. These airports, with an average of 32 based aircraft, account for 38 percent of the Nation's general aviation fleet. These airports are the most convenient source of air transportation for about 19 percent of the population and are particularly important to rural areas.

In 1964 a new, modern terminal and tower complex replaced LaGaurdia's original terminal, which had become quaint and dysfunctional with age. The original hangars eventually also gave way to additional new terminals.

O'Hare provided an effective, inexpensive mass-transit link to the city it served. Unusual for the time, Ralph Burke had included a rail link to the Chicago Loop in his plans for the airport, and his successors kept that link in the revised plans.

Mayor Daley, Chicago's answer to New York's Mayor LaGuardia, took a keen interest in O'Hare's development, and got the city's $155 million share of the costs financed by airport revenue bonds at no cost to local taxpayers.

O'Hare took well to its elevated role. It soon became the nation's busiest airport, and within five years it reached full capacity. The stage was set for further expansion that would practically turn O'Hare into a perpetual construction site, a fate it shared with most of the nation's major airports.

Los Angeles Airport's entry into the jet age also required substantial facility improvement. Its runways, which had been extended to 8,000 ft in 1953, could handle the early jets under most conditions, but

needed to be further extended to comfortably cover all takeoff contingencies for the longest range flights. American Airlines started jet service at Los Angeles in January 1959, with transcontinental service to New York. By the following September, one runway was extended to 10,000 feet, and a year later the other one was lengthened to 12,000 feet.

An equally important priority was the construction of a new, modern terminal. The airport was still struggling with the ones built temporarily in the 1940s. The development of the master plan that brought the airport into the jet age had been underway since the mid 1950s, and in 1956 a $59 million bond issue was completed to fund it.

In 1961 the jet age terminal complex Los Angeles so badly needed was finally completed. The main building was an enormous, long, functional structure placed squarely between the two recently extended runways. Passengers checked in at the main terminal and boarded their aircraft in oval-

The terminal that most caught the popular imagination in the jet age was TWA's futuristic looking terminal at JFK, completed in 1963. In spite of its appearance, it was scaled for propliners and had an old-fashioned horizontal layout that was problematic throughout its active service.

Below: The swirling, soaring interior of TWA's terminal at JFK left passengers in | no doubt that they were going flying.

shaped satellite terminals located on the tarmac. The terminal complex completed the conversion of the airport into one of the world's most modern and largest jetports and was dedicated with great fanfare by Vice President Lyndon B. Johnson.

While the terminal and runways were the important substantive elements of the transformation of Los Angeles International Airport, in the public eye it came to represent the jet age because of a unique, eccentric structure, the Theme Building. Placed in front of the terminal on the landside, it resembles a spidery flying saucer that is straight out of *The Jetsons*. Crossed, 135-foot-high parabolic arches support an elevated disk that contains a restaurant and an observation desk and looks as if it had just made a soft landing from Jupiter or Mars. Built by William Pereira, it may have been in part inspired by his brother Hal, who was art director of the acclaimed 1954 science fiction movie *War of the Worlds*.

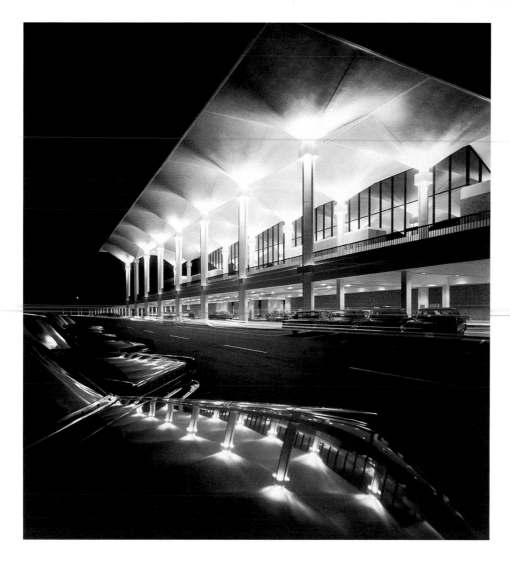

The Modern Style was the "in" look in the early 1960s, and it wasn't restricted to the major airports. Memphis Airport's new terminal was completed in 1963.

The Theme Building has become one of the landmark buildings of Los Angeles and was fully renovated in 1997. The restaurant was re-launched as the Encounter Restaurant, with an interior theme designed by Walt Disney Imagineering. It has a very retro sci-fi look complete with lava lamps, moon-cratered walls, metallic bar counter, calico carpet, electric-colored martinis, and silver space suit-clad waitstaff. It is the only restaurant at a major U.S. airport today that attracts a large clientele from the local community who come not to travel but only to eat.

The airport that most came to symbolize the modern jetport as jet service entered its second decade was Dallas/Fort Worth International Airport. Its detailed planning commenced in the

mid-1960s, and it was completed in 1973. It was the world's biggest airport, covering 17,500 acres of prairie land and costing over $700 million.

Its creation was a Texas-sized story of feuding and intrigue between Dallas and Fort Worth reaching all the way back to 1927. The two cities are 34 miles apart, which has always made a joint airport a logical consideration. But when Dallas first suggested it in 1927 and Fort Worth rebuffed the notion, the two cities stubbornly went their separate ways for the next four decades. Dallas had Love Field, purchased from the army in 1928, and Fort Worth built Meacher Field and later the grandly named Greater Southwest International Airport.

The two cities' choice of independent airports posed no problems until 1940, when they both requested substantial federal funds, which the CAA saw as wasteful duplication. The feuding continued anyway, but as the jet age dawned, the federal government found neither airport suitable for expansion to fully meet the area's needs. In 1964 the FAA put its foot down, and the cities had no choice but to cooperate if they were to receive additional federal funding for an airport. It was an arranged marriage, but it has worked spectacularly well.

It is the classic jetport, with the terminal complex placed between two sets of 12,000-foot parallel runways. It also has two remote crosswind runways and is so large that it is the only airport in the world requiring three simultaneously operating control towers to handle its traffic.

Dallas/Fort Worth's six terminals are arranged as three sets of semicircular structures with the access road running between them. The modular terminals efficiently concentrate the number of gates in the assigned space. However, it can be an ordeal for passengers—especially those with tight connecting flights—to traverse the distance between gates at opposite ends of the terminals, or between different terminals. The problem is alleviated by an easy-to-use monorail that connects the terminals. Dallas and Tampa were the first two U.S. airports to be equipped with monorail systems in the early 1970s.

Dallas/Fort Worth, home base for American Airlines and a major hub for Delta, handled 200

million passengers in its first decade, and that was before deregulation really took off. In 1998 for the first time over 50 million travelers passed through DFW in one year, and it vies with Chicago O'Hare and Atlanta Hartsfield for the title of the nation's busiest airport. It serves over 40 airlines, is a major international hub to Central and South America, and also provides direct flights to Europe and Asia. DFW has tremendous potential to expand, with the possibility of constructing new and redeveloped terminals with 100 gates each.

Many airports expanded significantly if not flashily to cope with the arrival of the jet age in the 1960s. Most engaged in runway lengthening and the construction of new terminals, many along the free space ringing the oval-shaped access road loop that had become a popular layout during the rapid

expansion of airports in the propliner era.

San Francisco International Airport got new terminals and runway extensions on more land reclaimed from the Bay. Its finger pier gates began to spread and would eventually look like an exotic complex of mazes from above, as the airport sought to make maximum use of the available space. Hartsfield Atlanta got a new Jet Age terminal in 1961, but within a decade that structure would be heading for obsolescence as the field became the fastest growing airport in the nation. And TWA's maintenance base on 4,300 acres of sprawling farmland north of Kansas City was transformed into Kansas City International Airport with a new terminal complex in 1972 to relieve obsolete, cramped Kansas City Downtown Airport.

While many airports underwent massive development in the early 1960s, by the end of the decade

An overhead portrait of Bellevue Airport in Washington state in 1966 shows the ominous encroachment of development that strangled to death many small airports, particularly near large urban centers.

the national system of airports couldn't keep up with the even greater growth in air traffic brought on by the jets. The 55 million passenger miles flown by all airlines in 1963 had shot up to 155 million passenger miles by 1969.

Such a flood of passengers overwhelmed the system. Delays became endemic. Aircraft spent hours in holding patterns over the major airports. Passenger dissatisfaction became a national topic of discussion, frequently featured in the media.

Compounding concerns about airport capacity was the introduction of the first widebody airliner, the Boeing 747 jumbo jet. It could carry as many as three times the number of passengers than its narrowbody predecessors. It was anticipated that at peak times, a rush of fully loaded 747s could easily overwhelm the passenger facilities of the largest airports and cause traffic jams on the taxiways.

Additional airport capacity was sorely needed, but the costs of modernization were reaching such large amounts that the established airport and airway financing mechanism was having difficulty keeping up with the demand for funds. JFK, the prototype modern jetport, consumed $100 million (exclusive of expenditures on the terminals); Dallas/Fort Worth, then under construction, was heading for $700 million.

Airport revenue bonds accounted for the local share of these costs, but it became clear that the future level of federal funding required would exceed the sources available from general federal tax funds. For the decade of the 1970s it was projected that $11 billion would be needed to improve and expand just the airports. The time had come to make airport and airway development self sufficient.

The federal government's solution was the Airport and Airway Development Act of 1970 and the accompanying Airport and Airway Revenue Act of 1970, which switched the source of federal funding for airports from the Treasury's general tax revenues to user fees drawn from the aviation community. These new sources of funds included a tax on all domestic airline tickets, a surcharge on international tickets originating in the United States, a tax on aviation fuel, a tax on air freight, and aircraft registration fees.

These revenues were to be collected into a national Airport and Airway Trust Fund which was to be under the jurisdiction of the Federal Aviation Administration. The arrangement was similar to the way interstate roads are financed by the Highway Trust Fund. As constructed, it was estimated that the total package would raise $11 billion over ten years. The big advantage of this system was that it provided a reliably predictable source of funding for airport and airway development that didn't have to compete with other government programs for allocations from the Treasury's general funds.

Parallel to funding from the federal trust fund, airports also continued to receive funding from state and local sources for terminal and landside projects, primarily through airport revenue bonds. In this regard the system was a continuation of the federal-local funding partnership established in 1938.

Over the years, the funding structure established by the Airport and Airway Development Act of 1970 has been fine-tuned in successive acts with the benefit of experience, but has fundamentally remained the mechanism of federal funding of the airport and airway system to the present. Since 1982, money has been disbursed from the trust fund under a capital grant program called the Airport Improvement Program, or AIP in the alphabet soup jargon of Washington.

Since 1982 the Secretary of State for Transportation also has been required periodically to publish a National Plan of Integrated Airport Systems, or NPIAS. This report, which looks five years into the future, is a planning document that covers all present and future airports deemed important to the national transportation system and eligible for AIP funding.

Following the 1970 restructuring of the financing of airports and airways, the industry entered an unexpected and prolonged period of economic difficulty caused by the oil crisis of 1973 and a decade-long period of double digit inflation. There was a dramatic dip in air traffic of all types due to soaring fuel prices and reduced real incomes that lowered demand for air travel.

This took some of the pressure off airport development, but it also reduced the growth in available

A view of Denver Stapleton Airport's tower behind a Western Airlines Boeing 720. Stapleton served the city well for decades, but it proved unsuitable for further expansion. This led to the construction of Denver International Airport.

The International Arrivals Building became a symbol of JFK and was used in many ads, including this one for Convair's newest jet.

funds. Congestion eased, and some major airport projects did come to fruition. But in the eyes of the public the typical airport terminal remained a drab, often crowded, unfriendly place, and more upheaval was to follow.

A bright spot for Newark was completion of its new jetport and terminal complex in 1973. It was essentially a brand new airport on vastly increased land area. The new terminal featured a cluster of circular satellite terminals for boarding. This was not the ideal layout for expansion of the existing facilities, but ample space was available for adding new buildings.

By the mid 1970s the frustrating inefficiencies and high costs caused by the bureaucracy of big government was giving rise to a growing movement that called for wholesale deregulation throughout the economy. In 1978, in one of its boldest and to this day most controversial policy changes, the government deregulated the airlines. The regulators had concluded that the industry was sufficiently developed to withstand competition and provide passengers less expensive air travel at a lower cost than it could under regulation.

On a phased schedule, within a few years all price controls, route awards, and flight frequency limits were removed. The airlines were completely free to fly anywhere in the U.S. at any level of frequency they desired, at any ticket price they saw fit to set. The only restrictions placed on access to airports were capacity limits based on the number of flights an airport could handle. Airlines could be started by anyone who could meet the FAA's requirements for airline operations, and they were free to compete with everyone else.

Deregulation turned upside down the staid world of the major airlines, whose financial and fleet structures were defined by the old world order. Airlines originally dominant in their markets attempted to consolidate their hold by fiercely competing with new entrants on price and service frequency, and embarked on ambitious route expansion themselves.

Mad dashes for market share ensued, triggering vicious price wars that eventually mauled the losers, but allowed the winners breathing room only until the next assault. Low-cost carriers were formed who found a pool of surplus pilots eager to work at any wage, and made life difficult for the majors on selected routes with cut-rate fares.

The industry quickly discovered that prices were the decisive factor in choice of carrier. Fare struc-

Business as usual at JFK's International Arrival's Building. Jets from over 40 countries appeared daily at the terminal in its last days before it was replaced by Terminal 4.

Below: Los Angeles International Airport's international terminal is shown in the early days, when airlines were already operating jets on long-range routes but still used propliners on short- and medium-haul flights.

tures became as complicated as the wiring diagram of a nuclear-powered aircraft carrier, and customer service suffered. Clever passengers able to plan ahead might pay only $200 round trip for a coast-to-coast flight and could find themselves sitting next to someone with less flexibility in travel planning who had paid $2,000 for the same trip.

All the airlines had close scrapes with profitability, but the well-managed, most powerful ones retained their dominant positions and grew stronger. United and American Airlines continued to vie for the top two spots in the industry, in spite of some scary swings in their financial fortunes, and expanded their route networks aggressively. Well managed Northwest hung on and expanded. Delta became a strong national contender by judiciously merging with Western Airlines. Several small regionals joined forces to form U.S. Air and carefully nurtured it into a national airline. Others

The Denver TRACON, controlling approaches and departures at Denver International Airport, looks like it could dispatch and control armies of space ships to distant galaxies. The new airport opened up a major mid-continental bottleneck, thus considerably improving on-time performance throughout the airway system.

regionals, like Republic, PSA, and Piedmont, were absorbed by the majors.

But other members of the old guard were not so skilled or lucky. Eastern and Continental were taken over by corporate raiders intent on streamlining their high cost structures primarily through massive compulsory wage concessions from the workforce. They drove Eastern into bankruptcy and out of existence. Continental gave in after a debilitating fight and barely survived, requiring a decade to rebuild the employees' and shareholders' morale. Frank Lorenzo, the chief raider, was later banned by the courts for life from running an airline because of his nasty, hardball tactics that went beyond the limits of the law. But that did little good for the thousands of airline employees who had lost their jobs because of him.

Normally prudent Braniff Airlines' new management embarked on an ill-advised, flamboyant expansion spree and spiraled into spectacular bankruptcy and out of business. TWA lived from one

protective bankruptcy to another like a socialite from marriage to marriage. And the most imperial of them all, Pan American Airways, America's foremost international flag carrier, which had no domestic network and waited too long to acquire National, struggled for a decade and a half, weakening progressively, before it disappeared.

Among the brash, optimistic upstarts who drove the majors to distraction, Air Florida, People's Express, Midway, MGM Grand Air, and others have come and gone. Southwest has become a low-cost legend, America West has hung on for a long time, and Jet Blue is the latest success story. Commuters mushroomed, connecting hundreds of out-of-the-way local airports with hubs served by the national carriers. Comair, ASA, Air Wisconsin, Bar Harbor Airlines, and Mesaba are but a few who entered the market with varying degrees of success.

The deregulated airlines' fluctuating fortunes may have turned life into an uncertain roller coaster

San Francisco International Airport had reached its final stage of maturity by the 1980s. Additional terminals have flanked the original 1954 terminal building, and all have sprouted a maze of satellite terminals, extensions, and sub-terminals. Only the final piece of the puzzle is missing: the new, wavy glass and steel International Terminal that would close the loop across and above the ground access artery by millennium's end.

for hundreds of thousands of airline employees, but without any doubt deregulation has given U.S. customers the cheapest ticket prices and the most comprehensive route network in airline history.

As interest rates finally retreated below double digits and the 1980s kicked off two decades of unprecedented economic boom in America, deregulation led to a renaissance of the American airport. Free to fly to any destination, but faced with overcrowding at the traditional airports serving scheduled carriers, airlines quickly started using alternative, underutilized airports within the same metropolitan area.

San Francisco International Airport in 1929.

Who Is the Busiest of Them All?

Contending airports keenly vie for the title of busiest airport, but the criteria can be tricky. Should it be by number of aircraft movements, or by number of passengers? Should it include transiting passengers or only passengers who begin their journeys at the particular airport? Passenger numbers generally win out over aircraft movements in such contests, because they are thought to be the best measure of economic activity, the key factor for airport performance.

The figures airport officials like to quote usually include all passengers passing through the airport. It is a legitimate claim indicative of an airport's physical capacity. By this measure, Atlanta's Hartsfield airport is the busiest in the world. Here is the list of America's 25 busiest airports in the year 2000 by the total number of passengers handled:

	Airport	Code	No. of Passengers
1	HARTSFIELD ATLANTA INTL	ATL	80,162,407
2	O'HARE INTL	ORD	72,144,244
3	LOS ANGELES INTL	LAX	66,424,767
4	DALLAS/FT WORTH INTL	DFW	60,687,122
5	SAN FRANCISCO INTL	SFO	41,040,995
6	DENVER INTL	DEN	38,751,687
7	MCCARRAN INTL	LAS	36,865,866
8	MINNEAPOLIS/ST PAUL INTL	MSP	36,751,632
9	PHOENIX SKY HARBOR INTL	PHX	36,040,469
10	DETROIT METRO	DTW	35,535,080
11	G BUSH INTERCONTINENTAL	IAH	35,251,372
12	NEWARK INTL	EWR	34,188,468
13	MIAMI INTL	MIA	33,621,273
14	JF KENNEDY INTL	JFK	32,856,220
15	ORLANDO INTL	MCO	30,823,509
16	LAMBERT-ST LOUIS INTL	STL	30,561,387
17	LESTER B. PEARSON INTL	YYZ	28,930,036
18	SEATTLE TACOMA INTL	SEA	28,408,553
19	LOGAN INTL	BOS	27,412,926
20	LA GUARDIA	LGA	25,374,866
21	PHILADELPHIA INTL	PHL	24,918,276
22	CHARLOTTE/DOUGLAS INTL	CLT	23,073,894
23	HONOLULU INTL	HNL	23,016,542
24	CINCINNATI INTL	CVG	22,537,525
25	WASHINGTON DULLES INTL	IAD	19,971,260

Source: Skytrax Research

Airports such as Newark for New York City, Oakland and San Jose for the San Francisco Bay Area, Fort Lauderdale for Miami, Baltimore for Washington, D.C., and Burbank for Los Angeles experienced a strong revival of scheduled service. Most notably, Chicago-Midway once again became a thriving center of scheduled activity as low-cost carriers jumped at the opportunity to offer service from a location so convenient to downtown Chicago, and were later joined by the majors.

The carriers also developed new regional hubs at underutilized airports far from the congested traditional transit spots. Cincinnati, St. Louis, Salt Lake City, Charlotte, Memphis, Houston, Detroit, Albuquerque, Cleveland, Hartford, Providence, Raleigh Durham, Fort Myers, and others grew from relatively quiet regional fields into important hub airports.

A big early winner of deregulation was Atlanta's Hartsfield Airport. It had been struggling since the late 1960s with its inadequate 1961 terminal and had been expanding its runway structure in fits and starts, but contentious arguments dragged on about the choice of expanding the present airport or building a new one. A master plan realigning the runway system into parallel runways capable of handling the biggest jets gave the opportunity to create a modern mid-field terminal complex with massive capacity and was finally accepted by all parties as the best option.

The redevelopment was completed in 1982, just as deregulation kicked into high gear. The new terminal set a new standard for the modern jetport. Its main terminal handled passenger-processing formalities for both departing and arriving passengers, but did not provide any boarding gates. It was connected by a rapid-transit rail system to five satellite linear concourses that contained all the gates. The advantage of this system was optimizing the smooth flow of passengers. It avoided passenger congestion by removing from the main terminal everyone waiting for an airplane, leaving it free exclusively for check-ins and baggage retrieval.

The redeveloped Atlanta Hartsfield was designed to handle up to 55 million passengers. It soon overtook Chicago O'Hare as the world's busiest airport as post-deregulation traffic found it to be the ideal hub, and within a few years it was handling close to 50 million passengers.

Atlanta Hartsfield inadvertently anticipated the future. The tremendous growth in traffic that followed deregulation during the 1980s and beyond made it imperative that new airport facilities be built both at the traditional airports and the newly ascendant ones throughout the country.

Above: A detail image of San Francisco's terminal complex reveals how an original structure can mushroom beyond recognition. The terminal built in 1954 is the light tan rectangular building that has had a new extension grafted onto its back; another extension pushed out onto the ramp in front of it, and a new tower added which overshadows the original.

Left: American airports have a tradition of operating their own fire, rescue, and police units. Security has especially gained in importance since the emergence of the terrorist threat after the turn of the millennium.

Top: Atlanta Hartsfield International Airport is the world's busiest airport. It was the first U.S. airport to apply a layout featuring a separate main terminal at which no boarding takes place. This was designed to keep passengers flowing to five linear satellite terminals containing the boarding gates. The oval race track of Candler Field is long gone.

Bottom: Chandler Field near Atlanta was a race track before it was donated by the family that controlled Coca Cola to be developed as Atlanta's municipal airport. Today it is Hartsfield International, the world's busiest airport, handling over 65 million passengers a year.

marble-accented, gilded comfort, from skyscrapers and high-tech suburban office parks, to the new temple of quality consumerism: the upscale shopping mall.

The newly emergent social norm of striving for a sense of quality-driven well-being had a profound effect on airport terminal design. It gave rise to the post-modern signature terminal, the unique architectural *tour de force* that seeks to awe but also to transform the time spent in it from hours of empty tedium into a pleasant and even useful experience.

One of the first terminals to embrace this approach was the United Airlines terminal, or Terminal 1 at Chicago O'Hare, completed in 1988. Built by Murphy/Jahn, the successor firm to C. F. Murphy Associates, who completed the original development of O'Hare in the early 1960s, Terminal 1 replaced the original international terminal. It is really two parallel terminals, separated by a wide taxiway apron.

The long, linear, steel and glass terminals can handle up to 70,000 people a day, and are vaguely reminiscent of the grand late 19th century glass and iron exhibition halls and railroad stations. This is not by conscious design but commonality of purpose. Both move great numbers of people and both strive to maximize natural light. The soaring ceiling and barrel-vaulted roof structure also suggest the interior of a cathedral to some. The pilots, however, many of whom show a healthy disdain for excessively serious interpretations and get a different perspective of the arched, silvery glass structure from a distance as they taxi up to it, quickly took to calling it "the diner."

The two-story main terminal serves both airside and landside functions and also handles ticketing and check-in. As has become the common custom at high-volume terminals, departures are processed on the upper floor while arrivals are cleared through the lower level. The satellite terminal provides additional boarding gates. An underground tunnel connects the two terminals and eases covering the long distance between them with the aid of moving sidewalks.

One of the finest examples of the modern signature terminal is Washington National Airport's Terminal 2, completed in 1997. It is designed by Cesar Pelli, a disciple of Eero Saarinen, with whom Pelli worked on designing Dulles.

From the early 1980s American consumers became increasingly quality-conscious as personal incomes rose and productivity gains pumped out a relentlessly swelling mountain of consumer goods at increasingly affordable prices. Plastic and polyester were out. Leather, wood, and natural fabrics were in. Japanese auto makers offered the highest standards of quality to shake up shoddy Detroit and seriously dent its dominance of the automobile industry. Refined cuisine and a wine culture to match any in the world became positive cultural stereotypes. Eclectic post-modern architecture cocooned the consumer in glass and

Washington National is the airport that won't go away. It is woefully cramped for efficient modern airliner movements; it requires a twisting, non-standard approach path along the Potomac River to avoid built-up areas, and it is literally across the street from the Pentagon. But it is much too convenient for Washington's politicians and bureaucrats with its close proximity and direct Metro link to their seats of power. So, instead of building a rapid rail link to Washington Dulles Airport, they decided to triple National's passenger capacity with a grand new terminal.

Terminal 2 had to sympathetically integrate the original 1941 Art Deco terminal into the overall design, and, similar to the original terminal, it had to be a worthy representative of the nation's capital. Mindful of the chronic public criticism of dreary, insufferable airline terminals, Terminal 2's politically savvy commissioners also specified that it had to be especially passenger-friendly.

Cesar Pelli's design exceeded these expectations and specifications. Terminal 2 borrowed the most successful aesthetic and functional features of the original terminal, and built on them to create a structure of superb aesthetic standards.

Departing passengers arrive at the terminal on the upper level, entering what appears to be a hall of comfortably modest height topped by modular domes. As they step into the building they are in for a treat. The hall opens up forward and downward, and they realize they are on a balcony, looking at the Washington skyline and its monuments through a shimmering wall of glass, similar to the original terminal. The check-in counters are behind the passengers, up against the landside wall, offering the counter staff the same superb view during their time on duty.

Passengers next descend down into the main linear concourse of Terminal 2, a soaring, cross-vaulted hall, the glass wall of which provided passengers with their first glimpse of the skyline view. It is strongly reminiscent of an airy, high-gothic cathedral. To history buffs, the branded shops tucked away along its side evoke the medieval merchants who used to surround the great cathedrals. To others it conjures up their favorite shopping center, and makes the hours fly by in case of any unforeseen flight delays.

Three finger piers extend from the main hall and contain the terminal's 35 boarding gates. Arriving passengers proceed to a lower level to collect their baggage and exit the terminal. The Washington Metro station is a short walk away under a covered walkway. The terminal can handle up to 16 million passengers a year.

The largest modern airport project in the United States in recent times was the construction of Denver International Airport. The initial debate was over whether or not Denver Stapleton Airport could be expanded. Stapleton was badly congested, and it's the effect of that problem reverberated throughout the national airway system because

Fortunately, crash and rescue crews rarely get the chance to practice their skills in a real emergency, but keep their skills sharp by countless hours of practice.

This aerial view of Los Angeles International Airport in the late 1970s clearly shows the satellite terminal system in use since the 1960s. The Theme Building is also visible. The Concorde has been an occasional visitor on publicity and charter flights but has never provided scheduled service to Los Angeles because of opposition to its sonic boom over land.

Stapleton was a central transfer point for east-west traffic. If Stapleton caused delays, flights backed up throughout the system. The debate over expanding Stapleton started as early as 1977, indicating the long timeline such complex projects require. The conclusions were that Stapleton was beyond fixing, there was still plenty of open prairie land around Denver for a new airport, and the controversies that locating such a mega-project near a major population center would cause could be managed.

It took until 1989 to complete site selection and acquisition, complete project approval, and evaluate the architect's design for the new airport. The city's request was for the main terminal, the airport's focal point, to uniquely reflect Denver's local heritage. The design submitted was a glass and steel structure that resembled a 19th-century railroad station,

Boston Logan International Airport became a major hub and international gateway by 1986, when this image was taken. The close proximity of the Boston skyline across the Charles River may suggest a quick commute downtown, but at rush hour when most flights arrive and depart it could take an hour or more to get across the gridlocked Callaghan Tunnel under the river. A 15-minute ferry ride was one popular alternative, and a second tunnel opened in 2003. In addition, extensive redevelopment at Logan has considerably eased traffic pressures.

playing on Denver's historic position as a major railroad junction. While it was seen as an excellent design, it wasn't thought to be unique enough to give an unforgettable signature link to Denver. It was also forecast to cost $48 million over the $1.5 billion budget and would require more time to build than the construction schedule specified.

Denver's municipal authorities asked local architectural firm Fentress and Bradburn to come up with a less costly solution that was more specifically

Above: This image from the 1980s illustrates the reason why politicians were always loath to shut down Washington National Airport, regardless of congestion, safety issues, and, more recently, a significant security threat. Downtown is minutes away from the airport by the Metro.

Right: Terminal 2 at Washington's National Airport was designed by Cesar Pelli. While other airline signature terminals are more modern in their appearance, this one evokes the look of a cathedral.

linked to Denver in appearance. The company was given three weeks to complete the new proposal.

Fentress and Bradburn's solution was to redesign the terminal's roof, giving it the striking Teflon fabric tent cover which was less expensive, faster to build and certainly delivered the signature look. The design reduced the structural steel required from 300,000 tons to 30,000 tons. It brought the project schedule back on track. And it could evoke the snow-capped Rockies visible from the airport, Native American tents, a cluster of billowing clouds, or any number of other images, but whoever saw it would never forget Denver.

The Teflon tent design wasn't new. It had been used most notably at the airport in Jeddah, Saudi Arabia, and in a number of less prominent projects, but it was unusual enough to deliver the signature effect. The rest of the design was modeled on Atlanta Hartsfield. Located between the two sets of main runways, the main terminal handled all the formalities of arrival and departure. It was linked by a rapid-transit rail system to three sets of satellite concourses, where the gates were. Additional concourses could be added as demand required.

When construction got underway on Denver International Airport, it brought new controversies. The $1.5 billion budget ballooned to $5.3 billion. The airport opened a year and a half behind schedule because a high-tech automated baggage system literally ate the baggage. The project was plagued by accusations of cronyism serious enough to trigger formal investigations by the FAA, the FBI, the Department of Transportation, the Department of Justice, and the Securities and Exchange Commission, although the probes proved little wrongdoing.

When the airport opened in 1995, it stunned visitors not only with its aesthetic appearance but with its sheer size. At over 70,000 acres it was four times the size of Dallas/Fort Worth Airport, or twice the size of Manhattan. Its 33-story control tower was the tallest in the world. The tented main terminal covered an area the length of three football fields and had seven stories. Yet the sumptuously finished interior was partitioned to human scale, where passengers found it easy to feel comfortable. Aviation enthusiasts found another link to Denver in the main terminal. It was named the Elrey Jeppesen Terminal after the pioneering airline pilot and Denver native who invented the instrument airway and approach charts used by airline and general aviation pilots throughout the world.

And Denver International Airport worked. Beyond the teething problems it experienced in its first year of operation, it has considerably eased the air-traffic logjam that had come to characterize Denver. Its five new runways, its all-weather operations capability that allows three simultaneous streams of takeoffs and landings in instrument conditions, and a smooth processing of passengers have had their effect. It is estimated that Denver International Airport has increased the capacity and efficiency of the entire national airway system by approximately five percent, and far more for flights directly routed through Denver.

While Denver represented gigantism in airport development, other airports throughout the country reconfirmed that small can also be beautiful. With money abounding throughout the economy during the 1990s and a new aesthetic demanding higher architectural standards, many smaller municipalities

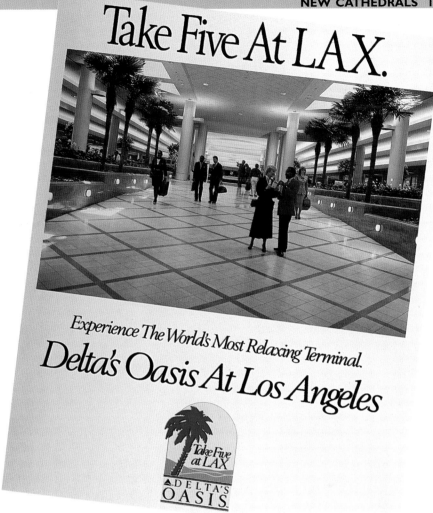

chose to upgrade their airport facilities, with pleasing results that succeeded in incorporating a distinctive local flavor. Particularly good examples are new terminals at the municipal airports of Lynchburg, Virginia; Chattanooga, Tennessee; and Nantucket, Massachusetts.

As civil aviation progresses in the United States into the 21st century, a few hyper airports along the lines of Denver International Airport may be built, but most airport capacity growth will come from the expansion and redevelopment of existing airports. Following years of financial wrangling and several false starts, New York's JFK was in the midst of a long overdue $9 billion redevelopment at the turn of the millennium. The terminals of Terminal City were being redone, or replaced with ambitious new facilities, and its inter-terminal transit system was also getting a major overhaul.

In the 1980s, Delta Airlines opened its own terminal at Los Angeles, Terminal Five, which it pitches in this innovative advertisement.

Left: Terminal 4 at JFK was developed and is managed by a private company, JFK IAT, under a lease from the Port Authority of New York and New Jersey. It is the first privately-owned, for-profit terminal in the United States. Sources of revenue include gate leases, services to the forty-plus airlines that use the terminal, and retail space leases. The experience so far suggests that it is a model worth following.

Of all the ongoing projects at JFK, its new Terminal 4, which replaced the famous but obsolete International Arrivals Building, is perhaps the best harbinger of the future airport, particularly the expectation of increasing ties to the private sector.

Airport authorities have long searched for ways to increase private sector involvement in airport management, counting on the efficiencies of privately run businesses to deliver more effective customer service. Certain concessions, such as food and beverage sales, cleaning services, and airport retail stores have long been subcontracted with mixed results, determined by the degree of competition in each situation. Airport security screening had been subcontracted for many years until the failures to intercept the hijackers of September 11, 2001, put airport security back into federal hands and off limits to private contractors.

JFK's Terminal 4 takes private-sector involvement to a whole new level. It is the first terminal that was developed and is fully managed on a turnkey basis by a private company hired by the airport's managing entity, the Port Authority of New York and New Jersey. The company is JFK IAT (JFK International Air Terminal), a joint venture founded by the Netherlands' Schiphol Group, which pioneered the transformation of airport concourses into retail malls; LCOR, a U.S. real estate developer; and Lehman Brothers, a U.S. investment bank.

Two factors are key to the success of the turnkey private sector management of an air terminal. First, it

Kennedy's current control tower is typical of the symbolic statements major airports have come to make with their control towers. It is one of few opportunities for airports to draw attention to themselves, and they rarely miss the chance. Newark, Chicago, Los Angeles, and Dallas/Fort Worth are among the airports that have distinctive towers.

has a single point of management authority to make all decisions, which provides great flexibility to meet changing requirements efficiently. Second, it is motivated by putting customer service first because customer dissatisfaction threatens the turnkey contract and the very survival of the management company.

It was a bold step by the Port Authority to completely hand over Terminal 4 to JFK IAT, and it appears to be a great success. A project on the scale of the new terminal could be reasonably expected to take ten years to complete based on past experience with airline terminal construction. JFK IAT projected that it would take five years and completed it on schedule. The terminal was budgeted at $1.2 billion, an impressive sum compared to the $100 million that the entire original JFK airport cost to develop, but it would not have been unreasonable to expect increases in the budget as the project progressed. JFK IAT completed the terminal on budget.

A particular challenge of constructing Terminal 4 was having to build it on the site of the IAB terminal without shutting down the old facility and interfering with passenger traffic during construction. This objective was smoothly accomplished by a carefully stage-managed segmented construction schedule. No section of the old terminal was shut down for demolition until a segment of the new terminal was available to accept its passenger flow. A complicated coordination of the resurfacing of the apron around the terminal was also required.

Terminal 4 is a U-shaped post modern glass and steel structure. The main building, to which JFK IAT refers as the headhouse—a term borrowed from the late 19th-century grand railroad station, when travel was an exotic adventure—consists of two cavernous halls: a ticketing check-in main hall and an adjacent shopping mall that is four city blocks long. It is awash with natural light both to provide passengers a comforting sense of a natural environment and to minimize the expense of operating artificial lighting.

Two gate concourses complete the U-shaped layout of Terminal 4 and offer 16 boarding gates. The terminal has been designed to easily expand to double its size without any disruption to the currently completed section, which serves over 40 airlines. A $1.6 billion Phase II expansion had been

on the way, with Delta Airlines destined to be its anchor client, but these plans have been scuttled by the latest economic downturn.

To enter the shopping mall, it is not necessary to pass through the security stations, which enables everyone, including non-passengers, to spend time in the stores and food and beverage outlets. While highbrow architects and cultural critics are bothered by the mallification of the airline terminal, the vast majority of people who have to spend time at airports are delighted by that trend, and JFK IAT is in the consumer satisfaction business.

Incoming passengers are served by a battery of passport control and customs stations on a lower floor. The terminal is the only one open 24 hours a day for customs and immigration services in the New York City area for. The baggage retrieval area is located beyond customs and provides access to another feature of JFK's redevelopment, the inter-terminal AirTrain, which will eventually connect to the Long Island rail services and finally provide JFK with a relatively inexpensive and fast rail link to Manhattan.

The most interesting aspect of Terminal 4 is how it differs from the International Arrivals Building of a previous generation, completed in 1957, which it replaced. The IAB provided mini-terminal areas to all of its client airlines, which provided each area

Denver International's dimensions are monumental, as were its cost overruns and its problem with its automated luggage handling system for which it got pilloried in the popular press. The media devoted considerably less attention to the airport's great utility to Denver and the entire transcontinental transportation system, because Denver International unblocked a bottleneck of delays caused by the obsolescence of its predecessor, Denver Stapleton.

The Ultimate Portable Airport

The most specialized airport is the modern, nuclear-powered aircraft carrier. It is a 1,100-foot airstrip from which 40-ton supersonic fighter bombers can take off and land simultaneously in any weather, day or night. It can be propelled along at over 30 knots by its nuclear reactors, which don't need refueling for five years in normal use. It can reach the remotest corner of any ocean faster than anything else afloat. Its typical complement of 85 warplanes can put on an air war far beyond the capabilities of the entire national air force of most countries. It is the ultimate portable airport, and the United States Navy has eleven of them.

The aircraft carrier's origins date back to aviation's earliest days. In 1910 Eugene Ely, a pushy barnstormer, succeeded in convincing the navy's first director of aviation to let him experiment with shipboard operations. Ely first performed a takeoff in his Curtiss Pusher off the coast of Virginia from a crude 85-foot wooden ramp built on the forecastle of the cruiser USS *Birmingham*. It was a scary performance, almost plunking Ely in the drink, and was written off as a stunt by the navy's top brass. But it was enough to gain skeptical agreement to a further experiment.

The navy built a longer ramp on the cruiser USS *Pennsylvania*, equipped with a critical innovation, the first arresting cables.

Eugene Ely accomplishes the first landing of an aircraft on a ship when he touches down on the specially prepared deck of the USS Pennsylvania in 1911 in San Francisco harbor. Note the arresting cables, which he hooked with a tail hook just as they do today.

They were lines of rope laid across the ramp, secured to 50-pound sandbags on each side. When Ely swooped in over San Francisco Bay for a landing on January 11, 1911, his experimental tail hooks down, they worked like a charm. The hooks snagged the lines and Ely's Curtiss ground to a halt in only 30 feet. After lunch, the ropes were removed and Ely buzzed off the ramp back to the airfield from where he had come.

In spite of Ely's successful demonstration, it took another decade for the U.S. Navy's conservative admirals to be convinced, ceding the development of the first aircraft

with a strong separate identity but was not an efficient use of space considering the small number of daily flights per airline. Terminal 4 has four generic check-in islands that provide 144 check-in stations, which can be set up with a few computer key strokes to represent any airline. The IAB was accessed from a single level roadway. Terminal 4 has multilevel access, including a new inter-terminal train link.

Terminal 4 embodies the progress air travel and the American airport have made in a century of flight. Daily it welcomes mammoth airliners flying in from every continent, each carrying a number of passengers greater than the entire annual passenger load of many fledgling airlines in the 1920s. The passengers Terminal 4 sends on their way can reach the farthest destination from New York in 22 hours of flying time.

The USS *Abraham Lincoln* after the September 11, 2001, terrorist attacks on the United States is ready to settle the score.

freeing up space on the aft section of the flight deck. But when the high performance jets came into service, the only way they could take off was by catapult launch. Following World War II, the flight deck layout was changed to give the carrier two runways at an angle to each other, permitting simultaneous aircraft launches and landings, or simultaneous launches from two runways.

The modern *Nimitz*-class carrier, such as the *Abraham Lincoln*, prowls the oceans at the head of a formidable battle group that includes guided missile cruisers, destroyers, frigates, resupply ships, and submarines. It is a self-contained town of over 5,000 inhabitants with its own postal zip code, TV and radio stations, newspapers, fire department, library, hospital, stores, barbershops, and more. It generates enough electricity to light 100,000 homes, it can distill 400,000 gallons of fresh water a day from the sea, and can function for 90 days without being resupplied.

On its 4.5-acre flight deck, its giant "Fat Cat" steam catapults accelerate the heaviest navy jets from zero to 180 knots the length of a football field in three seconds and can launch four aircraft a minute. The arresting cables trap jets touching down at 150 knots and stop them in less than 400 feet in two seconds. Eugene Ely would be impressed.

carriers to the British. The first operational U.S. carrier was the USS *Langley*, a converted collier put in service in 1922. By 1928 it was joined by the USS *Lexington* and USS *Saratoga*, both equipped with 900-foot-long flight decks. The three carriers could field 200 aircraft, including the most modern fighters and torpedo bombers.

The portable naval airport came into its own in World War II, particularly in the Pacific, where in large measure the war was fought from Japan's and America's carriers in such epic engagements as Pearl Harbor, the Coral Sea, and Midway. An aircraft carrier even launched a contingent of U.S. Army B-25 bombers 700 miles from Tokyo in 1942 for a surprise raid against Japan in symbolic reprisal for the devastating carrier-launched attack on Pearl Harbor.

The launch catapult, the other key carrier innovation besides the arresting cable system, came into widespread use during World War II. Initially catapults were employed to make operations more efficient by speeding up launches and

Although startling in appearance and an eye-catching architectural achievement, Terminal 4 is also ordinary, in the way that a railroad station was ordinary back when every airline flight was a heroic adventure. It is a pristine, glowing, space-age structure, not self-consciously designed to be one like the 1963 TWA terminal next door, but appearing as it does because it is the most expedient and efficient way to construct the effective, comfortable, and aesthetically pleasing style of terminal that the traveling public has come to take for granted.

Aviation has always espoused going farther, faster, and higher, with little inclination to look behind. Yet, as we celebrate a century of flight and look uneasily into the future as the deregulation-induced financial and economic upheaval among the airlines continues, there are also increasing opportunities for the occasional glimpse at our airports' past. The TWA terminal at Kennedy is in a sad state of repair, but it has escaped demolition, and momentum is building to properly preserve it.

At nearby LaGuardia the Marine Air Terminal continues to thrive as an airline terminal. The flying fish still gleam along its exterior, and in a quiet moment before embarking on a flight it is not difficult to conjure up a Boeing flying boat, engines running, ready to taxi out onto Flushing Bay and commence its takeoff run on the long haul to the Azores or Bermuda.

Newark, LaGuardia's old archrival across the Hudson River, has long ago reclaimed the title of busiest airport in the greater New York area, as it had been in the 1930s before Mayor Fiorello LaGuardia took exception and created the airport named after him. In tribute to its historic past, Newark has recently refurbished Building 1, the old Art Deco terminal that crowned that airport's leading position back in 1930.

Another old terminal still in regular airline use is Washington National Airport's original terminal. It is destined for a comprehensive historic preservation, but as with so many airport projects before, that work has been delayed by the economy's unfavorable state.

At Los Angeles International Airport seekers of the past can always have a meal atop the Theme Building and revel in the 1960s atmosphere. To go further back in time they can go to the cargo terminal area, where they'll find the old Spanish Revival hangar and lean-to terminal built in 1930 when the airport was still Mines Field, better known for air racing than as a field serving the airlines.

Should you find yourself at Cheyenne Airport in Wyoming, you might want to glance at the old United hangar and the terminal from the 1920s, when Cheyenne was as important a stop for United as Denver is today.

Other signs of airports past can be found where airplanes no longer fly. Glendale's famous terminal still stands in the industrial park the airport became when it was overtaken by development. Pan American's famous Dinner Key terminal is Miami's city hall today. Albuquerque's adobe terminal survives as home of the city's Junior League, which is committed to its preservation.

And at Wright Patterson Air Force Base, after too long an interval, visitors can once again view Huffman Prairie, where the Wright brothers really learned to fly in the summer of 1904 and set in motion the events that led to the Boeing 747 and the global jetports in less than a lifetime.

America's latest major airport to be built, Denver International Airport rises from the prairie as if it were a community gathering of Native American tents. Other interpretations evoke the Rocky Mountains, clouds, and meringue.

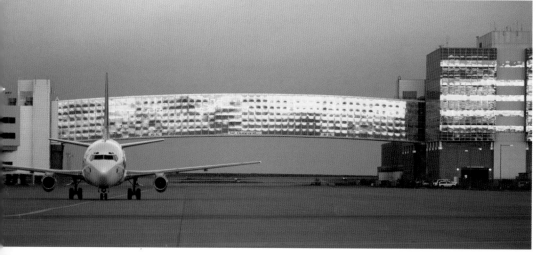

The bridge between the main terminal and the first satellite terminal at Denver International is high enough to let airliners taxi under it. On a clear day, with a bit of imagination, you can pause on it and see all the way to Huffman Prairie.

Index